AUSPICIO REGIS ET SENATUS ANGLIÆ
10,000 ft
Kotal
Dalikeh
Kergo Is.
Karrack Is.
Khoosh-ab
Borasjoon
Chahkota
Bushire
Chagaduk
6,000 ft
Reshire
100
Halilah
HALILAH BAY

JOHN COMPANY'S LAST WAR

JOHN COMPANY'S
Last War

BARBARA ENGLISH

MANOHAR
2026

First published 1971
Reprinted 2026

ISBN 978-81-19139-52-1

Published by
Ajay Kumar Jain for
Manohar Publishers & Distributors
4753/23 Ansari Road, Daryaganj
New Delhi 110 002

Printed at
Replika Press Pvt. Ltd.

Contents

List of Illustrations

LIST OF ILLUSTRATIONS

MAPS

Prologue

The whistling of the pipes grew louder, the thudding of the drums and the men's feet through the streets. In the crowded harbour the fleet waited, steamships and sailing ships. Round the last corner the regiments suddenly appeared – tight neat uniforms with pillbox hats, brown faces gleaming in the false dawn before the Indian day. "John Company", the Honourable East India Company, the trading company which founded an empire and owned a continent, was going to war. At sunrise the men were embarked, men, horses and baggage being ferried out in small cotton boats. Groups of shivering native boatmen crouched watching, silhouetted against the golden sky. As the guns crashed out the salutes across the harbour, the ships sailed away from Bombay, in the year 1856, bound for Persia. It was John Company's last war, although no one knew it then; such a futile war, about a city no one in England had heard of, and a woman no one much liked.

Acknowledgments

The writing of this book has taken a long time, and during that time many people have helped me. I should like to record my gratitude to the Earl of Harewood, for permission to quote from Lord Canning's papers, and to Captain N. A. Ussher and the late Mr A. Walker for much kindness shown to me whilst I was working at Harewood: the Scottish Record Office and the Earl of Dalhousie: Lord Elphinstone: Sir Henry Havelock-Allan and the North Riding of Yorkshire Record Office: Mr H. T. Lambrick of Oriel College, Oxford (John Jacob's diary): Mr Edmond Combe of Richmond, Surrey (Cornet Combe's letters): Miss Beryl A. S. Hodder of Worthing (Assistant Surgeon Sylvester's diary): Major H. Barker of R.H.Q., Queen's Own Highlanders (Corporal Borthwick's letters): National Army Museum (papers of Surgeon John Mills and John Braithwaite Hardy): W. A. Thorburn of the Scottish United Services Museum: Mr Michael Maclagan of Trinity College, Oxford: the London Library: Mr F. G. B. Hutchings, formerly City Librarian of Leeds: the staff of the India Office Library: Major H. Butterworth of R.H.Q., The Staffordshire Regiment: the British Museum: Mr Richard Collier: Sir Fitzroy Maclean: Mr D. Gourlay of Aberdeen: my husband (who helped with the maps) and my sons. Unpublished Crown copyright material in the India Office Records transcribed in this book appears by permission of the Secretary of State for Foreign and Commonwealth Affairs.

CHAPTER ONE

The Fabled City of Herat

FROM a long way off the city was visible. It lay in the plain under the Paropamisus mountains, and the whole plain was full of little villages, gardens, vineyards and cornfields, cut through by small irrigation streams gleaming under the sun in the clear light of Central Asia. Here the inhabitants harvested corn, herded sheep and goats, and grew thirty-two different sorts of grape, the marble and raisin grape, the golden grape of Cas-vine, and the small red grape of Budduckshan.

The city was the city of Herat in the middle of the nineteenth century, the capital of a rich province lying in the wastes of Central Asia, isolated, yet astride the conqueror's route to India. On the plain where the city stood, the great roads from all the principal countries of Asia meet, from Persia, from Russia, from Afghanistan and India. Of the foundation of Herat nothing is known, although because of its antiquity and importance it was always said (as was anything ancient and important in Central Asia) to have been founded by the great Alexander. Its massive walls dominated the plain and had done so from time out of mind – twenty-five foot walls standing on a huge earthwork two hundred and fifty feet thick – who else but Alexander could have built such a city? In every age, under every dynasty, Herat played a part in the history of Central Asia. It was sacked by Jenghiz Khan and by Tamerlane. Between the twelfth and seventeenth centuries, Herat was devastated at least seven times. But every time the people returned, the fields were cultivated again, and the buildings arose out of the ruins.

Six hundred miles east of Teheran, and as far to the west of India's North-West Frontier, Herat was virtually unknown to Europeans. Even Persia was the unknown, the mysterious East, but at least Europeans went there, wrote books, conducted diplomatic missions and traded: but east of Persia very few travellers ever went, and not all of them came back. Britain went to war to protect Herat – India sent subsidies to assist Herat – Russia and Persia were very interested in acquiring Herat – but almost nothing was known of the city, and even its exact position was unknown to European cartographers. But this lack of knowledge did not mean lack of interest, and the government of Britain especially was continually anxious about Herat.

It was during the Napoleonic wars that Britain first began to fear for the North-West Frontier of India. In the year 1807 the Emperor Napoleon met the Emperor Alexander of Russia on a raft moored in mid-stream on the river Memel: within hours the British Foreign Secretary was considering their "secret" Treaty of Tilsit. The two emperors planned to attack British India by way of Constantinople, Asia Minor and Persia. The French threat disappeared with Napoleon, but the Russian threat persisted and overshadowed the Frontier for the whole of the century thereafter. Only on the North-West Frontier was India open to attack, and from the North-West, India's conquerors had always come. Above the Khyber Pass lay the provinces which later became Afghanistan, the only buffer state of any strength between British India and Russia. To the north of Afghanistan lay the Khanates, Merv, Khiva, Bokhara and Samarkand. Romantic names, Merv, once Queen of all the World, Khiva the forbidden city, Bokhara the capital of Tamerlane, and Golden Samarkand. The Khanates, all possessing glorious pasts, were now merely oases of independence which were being swallowed by the Russian advance. Beyond Afghanistan to the west was Persia, a decaying empire falling under Russian influence. In the debatable lands between Persia and Afghanistan lay the rich province of Herat.

For a time the attention of the civilised world was bent on Central Asia, this No-Man's-Land where the Russian and the British empires moved slowly towards each other, like two glaciers engulfing all the lands before them. Ahead of the armies came agents, spies, explorers, travellers, all engaged in "The Great Game", the struggle for imperial dominance played out by solitary men in some of the loneliest places of the world. "From the Caspian to the Karokoram and from the Khyber Pass to the confines of Siberia, throughout the whole of the vast but rapidly narrowing Tom Tiddler's Ground that separated their respective Empires, Englishmen and Russians, and men of other races and nationalities too, played what they and their contemporaries called The Great Game."[1] The advancing frontiers caused a Russian diplomat to remark to an Englishman, "If we go on at this rate, the Cossack and the Sepoy will soon meet on the banks of the Oxus." The reply came, "Very probably, Baron; but however much I should regret the collision I should have no fear of the result."[2]

In spite of these brave words, the British did in fact fear the result. Pamphlets poured from the private presses beloved of the amateur politicians of the nineteenth century:

"The Defence of our North-West Frontier" "England and Russia in the East" "Future and Policy of Britain as a Great Power", and many others of the same kind. The fear of Russia dominated all thinking about the North-West Frontier, and the importance of Herat was mentioned over and over again. The defences of Herat were truly formidable to the primitive siege trains available – those twenty-five foot walls, on a fifty foot earthwork, surrounded by a forty-five foot ditch could and did withstand months of siege. But whoever took Herat could march on the North-West Frontier of India – certainly it was still a long way to go, and through terrible country and treacherous tribes, but nevertheless it could be done.

To-day the Russians and the Americans play another "Great Game" in Afghanistan, not unlike that of the nineteenth-century Russians and Britons. The Russians have poured hundreds of millions of dollars into North Afghanistan, and are thought to have provoked Afghanistan's breach with Pakistan over "Pakhtoonistan", a projected independent state for the Pathans. The Americans concentrate chiefly on the Herat and Kandahar provinces, at a much smaller cost, some millions of dollars.

In the nineteenth century the Heratis thought of their city as the market place for Turkestan, Afghanistan, Persia and India: but the British called it the "Gate of India" or the "Key of India" because it was only by the Herat route that large armies, equipped with heavy artillery, could march on the North-West Frontier. North-east of Herat loomed the Hindu Kush, the highest mountains in the world: south lay the deserts of Baluchistan and Sind. But the province of Herat itself was so fertile that it was called the granary of Central Asia, and there were there also all the raw materials for war, iron, sulphur and lead, timber in abundance and saltpetre. Every conqueror of India had as a preliminary captured Herat.

The city itself was a divided one, and very often, true to the proverb, it did not stand. Both Persians and Afghans had at one time ruled Herat. The Heratis themselves were some Persian and some Afghan. The rulers of Herat and the soldiers were Sunni Moslems, and many of the shopkeepers and citizens were Shiah Moslems. Most of the Afghans were Sunnis and most of the Persians Shiahs. So loyalties in Herat itself tugged two ways – some Heratis were pro-Afghan: some for Persia. Many of both parties would have preferred independence from both Afghans and Persians.

The extreme ill-will that existed between Shiahs and Sunnis in the 1840s had to be seen to be believed. The difference between the two sects arose after the death of Mohammed, and while the Sunni revered Abu Bakr, Umar, and Uthman, the three men who were made caliphs after the death of the Prophet, the Shiah believed that the three caliphs were usurpers, and that the rightful caliph had been Ali, Mohammed's son-in-law. "May God curse Abu Bakr, Umar and Uthman, and shed his peace upon the blessed Ali!" was a common Shiah greeting: and the names of the caliphs were used in the insults the Shiahs hurled at their mules and each other, "May the face of the father and the father's father of your Umar be defiled." [3] The chief outward difference between the Sunni and the Shiahs that one Englishman noticed was that the Sunni washed from the tips of their fingers to their elbows, and the Shiah from their elbows to the tips of their fingers*:

* So rigidly adhered to was this rule that the Moslems claimed to

in fact he was as puzzled as an Afghan in England would have been to distinguish between a Roman Catholic and a Protestant.

The Afghan Sunnis considered it praiseworthy to hunt down Persian Shiahs, and sell them as slaves. If the captured Persians unfortunately turned out to be Sunnis, they could be tortured until they declared themselves Shiahs, when they could be sold with a clear conscience. The number of slaves existing in Central Asia was colossal – in 1844 the Emir of Bokhara had according to his own account 200,000 Persian slaves[4] and their value was very low. In the 1830s a horse was worth from twelve to fifteen male and female slaves; a good horse, later sold for £50, cost twenty-one slaves in Herat about 1840.[5] Herat in particular was a centre of the slave trade, and the capture and sale of Persians by the Heratis was to the Shah of Persia a constant excuse for war.

Before the mid-nineteenth century, few Europeans had seen Herat, and fewer survived to describe what they had seen there. Travelling was by camel or horse, and death could come in many ways – disease and bandits were the chief killers. Nevertheless several Europeans came through Herat between about 1800 and 1850, perhaps one European every decade crossed from Persia to India by the Herat route. These men were adventurers looking for a fortune, ex-soldiers seeking an army to command, deserters on the run or hopeful politicians gathering facts for their governments. There was too, a missionary spirit in some men, such as one who wrote *c.* 1840, "we are on the eve of stirring times; but

be able to distinguish between a Sunni and a Shiah by the way the hairs lay on their arms.

if we play the great game that is before us, the results will be incalculably beneficial to us, and to the tribes whose destinies we may change from turmoil, violence, ignorance and poverty, to peace, enlightenment and varied happiness."[6] Such men with such motives would to-day go to the wilder parts of Africa, but in the early nineteenth century they went to Central Asia.

Their courage was fantastic. They were usually very ill-equipped for their journeys – ignorant of the languages they would have to speak, only knowing through travellers' tales of the route they would have to follow. It was impossible to take much money, or good clothes, or even a good horse without inviting robbery. All map-making and even note-taking was dangerous, as the native tribes soon learnt that map-making by the British led all too often to conquest by the British. Religion was a danger too, for many fanatical Moslems would have thought it a good day's work to kill a Christian, even an inoffensive travelling companion.

The rewards of these fearsome journeys across Central Asia were uncertain. Some men, such as "Bokhara" Burnes and Eldred Pottinger became famous for the rest of their lives because of their adventures: others seemed to have passed by almost unnoticed: others still never reached their destination or never returned.

Of the men who travelled to Herat in the nineteenth century, one of the first was Captain Charles Christie of the Bombay Native Infantry, who came to Herat in 1808, and described the city, then in a very prosperous state, with great enthusiasm.[7] He was amazed by the cultivation of the foul-smelling asafoetida, which wa sgrown in all the plains and hills round Herat, and exported to Baluchistan and India. It grew to two or three feet high, had a stem two inches in diameter and a yellow head rather like a cauliflower. No amount of cooking seemed to kill its taste and smell.

In 1818, Gardiner, an Irish deserter who called himself an American, may have come to Herat, but his stories are more fabulous than real.[8] In 1826 an ex-officer of Napoleon's Imperial Guard, named Court, travelled across Afghanistan to the Punjab, and thirteen years later a translation of his journal, including a description of Herat, reached the Governor-General of India.[9] Court was accompanied by a colourful Neapolitan adventurer, Paolo di Avitabile.[10] About the same time Charles Masson travelled from Russia to India through Persia, Meshed and Herat. His adventures were terrifying, and it seems incredible that he survived – at one stage he was "without money or clothing, a stranger in the centre of Asia, unacquainted with the language which would have been most useful to me, and from my colour exposed on all occasions to notice, enquiry, ridicule and insult."[11] He did however, survive, and returned to leave his journals with the British Resident in the Persian Gulf before re-entering Central Asia for more punishment. The Resident thought that Masson was an American from Kentucky, but he was in fact a deserter from the Bengal Artillery who had been christened James Lewis. During Masson's absence on his second journey his journals were sent to the Government of India, much to Masson's annoyance, and used for furthering the political schemes of the Governor-General, Lord Auckland.

Masson wrote a very good description of Herat as he found it in the 1820s. In his time it was a walled city, containing a number of once fine buildings, now decaying. These were the ancient palaces and tombs of former kings, which were never repaired by their successors as they preferred to build anew. To the rich markets of the city came "Persians from Meshed, Moguls from Turbut, Tartars from Bokhara, Kurds, Afghans, Seistanees and Beloches."[12] The markets were full of the produce of the rich valley of Herat – apples, pears, almonds, grapes, peaches, apricots, cherries, quinces, melons, mulberries, pomegranates and pistachio nuts, cabbages, spinach, lettuce, carrots, turnips, radishes and onions. Manufactures were silk, worsted, woollens and carpets, swords, pistols and carbines. There were few cows but many camels, horses and fat-tailed sheep, the sheep being milked to produce butter and cheese. At this time (1826-8) the government of Herat was moderately efficient and the slave trade temporarily abolished, but within fifteen years the slave market was to be re-introduced.

In 1828, a Bengal civil servant, Edward Stirling, travelled through eastern Persia to India. At the time this journey roused no official interest: the information Stirling brought back was not wanted, and he lost his post because he had overstayed his leave.[13]

A year after Stirling made his journey, a young lieutenant in the Bengal Cavalry, Arthur Conolly, left Moscow for India in a snowstorm, and after many months reached Herat. The city itself lay "at four miles distance from hills on the north, and twelve from those which run south of it. The space between the hills is one beautiful extent of little fortified villages, gardens, vineyards, and cornfields, and this rich scene is lightened by many small streams of shining water, which cut the plain in all directions. A dam is thrown across the Herirud, and its waters, being turned into many canals, are so conducted over the vale of Herat that every part of it is watered . . . [the Herirud] is 'as clear as tears', and, the natives say, only equalled by the waters of Kashmir, which make those who drink them beautiful."[14] The town itself did not impress Conolly so favourably: he described it as one of the dirtiest in the world. It was roughly square, divided into quarters by four long bazaars covered with arched brick, which met in a domed quadrangle in the centre of the city. Many of the smaller streets were also covered in, and these tunnels were full of refuse, piles of muck with dead cats and dogs and even dead horses. As an inhabitant remarked: "but if dirt killed people, where would the Afghans be?"[15]

Three years after Conolly's visit, a young Indian, Mohun Lal, spent seven months in Herat whilst travelling through Central Asia with Europeans. He makes the province sound a paradise from the Arabian Nights, even the salt mines were "red, with white veins, shining like crystal." Once upon a time "the caravan of Bokhara, which came thrice a year, loaded with gold-sand and silver, greatly enriched this place, and the caravan of Persia annually supplied it with the shawls of Kirman . . . The whole of Afghanistan was plentifully supplied with gold mohurs coined in Herat, and also with many kinds of silk cloth . . . The carpets made of wool at Herat are extremely handsome; they are covered with open artificial flowers, in different colours. They are sent to Turkistan, and even to Afghanistan, with a great profit."[16]

Conolly had taken with him when he left Herat a Herati as a servant, who afterwards learnt medicine in Calcutta and then returned home. It was this man who one day in 1837 saw through the disguise of a young British officer in the bazaar of Herat.[17] He was Eldred Pottinger, whose name was always to be associated with Herat. He was then a twenty-six-year-old lieutenant in the Bombay Artillery, and had been encouraged to travel (unofficially) by his uncle, the Resident in Cutch, to collect information about Afghanistan, in which the Government of India was becoming interested for political reasons. He travelled as a horse dealer as far as Kabul, where he changed his disguise to that of an Indian Saiyyid (holy man) and went on to Herat. He used to silence criticisms of his strange religious observances (or non-observances) by explaining to the Afghans that these were the ways of Indian Moslems.[18] Apparently his disguise was quite convincing to the Heratis, except for the one man in Herat who had lived in Calcutta and knew what Europeans looked like. Later when more Europeans travelled in Central Asia, and when the visit of a European was too often followed by war and annexation, disguise had to be more thorough, and anyone with "green eyes" would be lucky to escape torture.

As soon as the Calcutta-trained doctor recognised Eldred Pottinger as a European he became very friendly and urged Pottinger to tell the Vizier of Herat who he really was. For the enemy was already threatening the gates of Herat – the enemy being the Persian army led by the Shah himself. Herat, under the divided rule of the weak Prince Kamran and the able but vicious Vizier Yar Mohammed, was likely to fall quickly: in fact Pottinger always believed that one English regiment could have taken it straightaway, and that even the Shah could have taken it in a day.

As the Persians advanced the Heratis withdrew, destroying the crops and cutting down and burning their trees as they went.[19] The Heratis thought the Persians contemptible cowards because they advanced in close order, defended by their guns, instead of straggling about to be cut off by the defenders. Nevertheless some Persian prisoners were taken, including the C.-in-C.'s secretary with all his papers.[20]

The ten-month siege of Herat which followed this Persian invasion of 1837 was a most curious affair. Pottinger, now revealed to all as a British officer, became the mainstay of the besieged Herat force as he considered it would be a disaster for India if the city fell. The Persian army too had British officers, one being the British Resident at Teheran, Colonel McNeill,[21] who had come with the Shah to dissuade him from attacking Herat. The two British officers of the two opposing armies met at the gates of the city for talks, Pottinger visited McNeill in the Persian camp, and McNeill called on the Prince of Herat and spent the night in the besieged city. It is not surprising that eventually McNeill, who constantly urged the Shah to give up the war, was obliged to withdraw from the Persian camp; his place as adviser was taken by a Russian officer who had supplied the Persians with Russian engineers and guns.

Eldred Pottinger had no practical experience of war at all, yet his theoretical training in siegecraft, and his refusal to accept defeat, were enough. Often it was only Pottinger who prevented the capture of Herat. He explained to the garrison what was happening when the Persians (under Russian guidance) began mining. He promised the Heratis financial aid from the British government (an offer repudiated by the Foreign Office). He tried to repress the more barbaric tricks of the defenders (the Persians were just as bad) expressing his disgust when Yar Mohammed paid head money to his soldiers – on the production of enemy heads. One day Pottinger was pleased to see Yar Mohammed caught out: a soldier got head money for a pair of ears, and soon after another tried for money for an earless head

– and both head and ears had belonged to a defender anyway.

Before long the siege brought great hardship to the defenders as food and fuel became scarcer and scarcer. Disease was rife among the narrow blind lanes of the city. But even when his citizens were at their lowest ebb, Yar Mohammed carried on his usual trick of torturing them to get money to pay his soldiers, or selling them off as slaves.

The turning point of the siege came on 24th June, 1838, six months after the Persians had encircled the city. On this day they actually breached the defences, and when Yar Mohammed and Eldred Pottinger hurried to the breach, the defenders were already scattering. Yar Mohammed thought all was up, and sat gloomily on the ground. Pottinger urged him up and on, and in face of the Vizier's reluctance began to shout at him and actually dragged him to the breach. Suddenly the Vizier found fresh courage and seizing a large stick he began to beat those defenders he could reach. More frightened of this attack than of the Persians in front, the Heratis leapt over the walls like goats and tore down the slope. The Persians turned and fled, and the city was saved, and was never thereafter in great danger. A factor in Herat's favour was that the Persian generals worked entirely independently of one another, "each being rather pleased if a rival general was defeated."[22]

Herat and Pottinger withstood the Persians for nearly ten months altogether. The Indian Government eventually acted, and sent a small force in two ships from Bombay two thousand miles to the Persian Gulf, to seize the small island of Karrack (now Kharg) at the westernmost edge of the Persian empire. News of the expedition reached the Shah in his camp outside Herat – but in transit the news of the two ships had snowballed to a force of 20,000 men. Thereupon Colonel McNeill sent his military aide, a slight, curly-haired youth with fuzzy side-whiskers, Charles Stoddart, with an ultimatum to the Shah. "If I don't leave Herat, there will be war, is not that it?" asked the Shah. "It is war," replied Stoddart, "all depends upon your Majesty's answer." After two days the Shah gave in, and on 9th September, 1838, Stoddart was able to report to McNeill that the Shah had mounted his horse and ridden away. He rode straight back to Persia with his army of 40,000 men and fifty guns, leaving the almost conquered fortress in ruins.[23] Eldred Pottinger was able to write to the government in Calcutta: "Thanks be to the almighty God I have the honour to report the cessation of hostilities in this quarter . . ."[24]

The British were left with the task of putting Herat together again. During the siege the population had dropped from 70,000 to 6,000 or 7,000[25] and by the end of the siege there was no food at all, and no crop had been sown. After the siege only within range of the sentries' rifles could crops be grown at all, for unprotected the crops and croppers were stolen by the raiding Turcomans. For some months Pottinger, now joined by Charles Stoddart, fed thousands of Heratis daily. Most of the city's revenue had formerly come from slave-trading, but after 1839 the Heratis were in no condition to capture slaves, and the British therefore kept the economy going by monthly subsidies to the Prince and chiefs. Nevertheless Yar Mohammed could not resist selling a few of his fellow citizens in exchange for horses and perhaps a little grain. His agents roamed the city trying to provoke the people into transgressing the laws, so that they might be sold. To keep out of trouble, the inhabitants spent as much time as they could in their homes: so then Yar

Herat about 1840; the tall towers are minarets

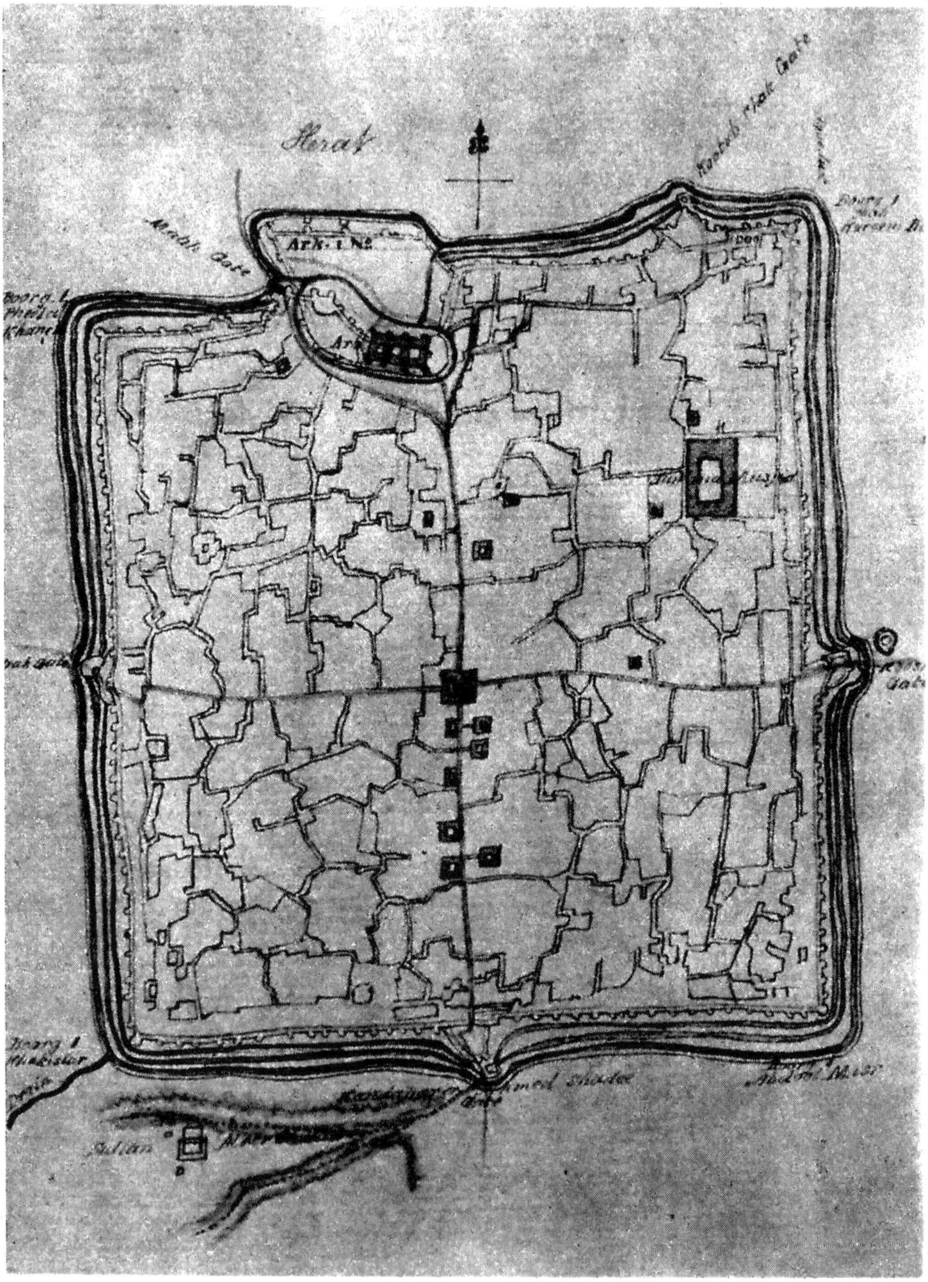
Herat

Part of the walls of Herat *c.* 1839

Plan of Herat *c.* 1839

The Hon. Charles Augustus Murray

Mohammed had to send troops to the bazaars at the most crowded time of day, to seize and sell those within reach.

Pottinger and Stoddart protested violently against this sort of thing, but their protests only made them unpopular. Stoddart left Herat two months after the end of the siege on a very unsuccessful mission to Bokhara, to try to persuade the Emir to give up his large numbers of slaves. Yar Mohammed's hostility followed him, for he sent a secret letter to the Emir describing Stoddart as a dangerous spy and suggesting that he be done away with immediately. Stoddart was thrown into the Black Well of Bokhara, which was stocked with specially bred vermin, including giant sheep-ticks and reptiles. Arthur Conolly (who had been to Herat earlier in the 1830s) came from India to rescue him, but only stayed to join Stoddart's imprisonment, and finally both were executed.[26]

For some months Pottinger stayed on alone in Herat, his relationship with Yar Mohammed gradually deteriorating. This man was now the real ruler of the city. The Prince, Kamran, had taken to drinking schnapps with a German adventurer, Dotterwich; Dotterwich was eventually expelled from Herat for insolence to Yar Mohammed, but the Prince continued to drink himself silly, egged on by his Vizier. An Englishman who travelled through Herat in 1840, described the ferocious ruffian Yar Mohammed then was, with only two remaining teeth, his long eye teeth, and his face with its rare unnatural smile and its "usual expression of quiescent malevolence."[27]

In March, 1839, Yar Mohammed began to negotiate with the Persians to evict the British[28] but the Persians cautiously sent the Vizier's letters to the British. In the opinion of the government of India Pottinger alone was no longer enough, and in July, 1839, he was replaced at Herat by a British Mission of six officers and four European N.C.O.s under Major D'Arcy Todd.[29] Pottinger was recalled to Calcutta, where he spent the next year trying to make up the accounts of his expenditure during the siege of Herat, and being nagged by the Government of India for his former extravagances and his inability to produce the proper receipts from Herat that the accountants demanded. He later played an important and dangerous role in the Afghan war of 1839-42, and died of typhus in Hong Kong at the age of 32.

The new British Mission began immediately to reform the amazed Heratis, who suddenly found themselves in a nineteenth-century Welfare State. All the able-bodied men who lacked work were employed in repairing the fortifications, and on reopening the many irrigation canals destroyed during the siege. Other families were set to spinning thread for carpets, and were paid for their work in flour. About thirty boys, rescued from slavery by Pottinger, were supported by the Mission and spent half their days learning a trade in the city and half at a special school set up for them. A dispensary and a hospital were opened, and a workhouse for the blind, lame and infirm, where incredulous visitors saw the blind taught to weave. Women were encouraged to make carpets again, a famous industry of Herat which was almost forgotten.[30]

The Europeans began to settle in. One of them, Captain Richmond Shakespear, was "thinking of putting coloured glass in my windows, and making other alterations in my quarters, as there appeared every prospect of my remaining at Heraut for many a day."[31] What would the Heratis have made of Victorian stained glass in their city? However, Shakespear was sent away to Khiva on a diplomatic mission, and soon the position of the officers remaining in Herat began to look less secure. Over them blew the restless wind of One Hundred and Twenty Days, which blows ceaselessly in Herat from June to September.

Slave-trading, the citizen's former employment, was absolutely vetoed by the British Mission, which was in a strong position because it controlled the purse strings. This was perhaps the beginning of the great dislike the ruler of Herat came to have for the Mission. But it was also something less tangible. The Afghans were to demonstrate to the unbelieving British time and again that they preferred independence to all the benefits of Western civilisation, and the Heratis were Afghans in this. "Their wretched country is a paradise in their eyes. They cannot believe that we desire their independence" wrote one officer with a wide experience of the lands above the Khyber Pass.[32]

Yar Mohammed would have liked the British subsidies without the British Mission, and so he began to intrigue with his former enemy the Shah (whom he addressed as "the Asylum of Islam"), with the Russians, with the Afghans and with the Khanates to the north. His intrigues were well-known to the British, and they were accompanied by both threats and by constant requests to D'Arcy Todd for larger subsidies and more cash. The British had already paid about £200,000 to the Herat government, and at a final demand from Yar Mohammed who "had been for some time in an habitual state of intoxication"[33] for an immediate payment of £20,000 and a greatly increased monthly allowance, Todd lost his patience and without waiting for his government's instructions withdrew his Mission to Kandahar in February, 1841. The Mission had scarcely left when the Residency was attacked and pillaged by a howling mob.[34]

Todd might have been forgiven, for he was in a very difficult position; it took a very long time for any answer to come to his letters to the government of India, and there was the added difficulty that Yar Mohammed stopped all Todd's couriers and read his letters at leisure. Stoddart had waited at Bokhara for the government's permission to withdraw, and he had been murdered when the British were defeated in Afghanistan. What chance was there that the Mission at Herat would have survived the Afghan war? Nevertheless the Governor-General Lord Auckland was furious that Todd had left Herat without orders, and Todd was remanded to his regiment in disgrace, declared unfit for further political employment.[35] He was killed during the Sikh wars.

Yar Mohammed was alarmed when he found the Mission had really left Herat, and expected a British brigade to march to Herat to recall him to his obligations. Instead he received two very friendly letters from the Indian Government, disowning all the later acts of Major Todd. Yar Mohammed and Herat, relieved of any further interference from the British, returned to their normal way of life, torturing and enslaving the wretched Shiahs. Between 1841 and 1849, the British were fully engaged in a disastrous war in Afghanistan, and a nearly disastrous war in the Punjab, and had little time or thought for Herat and Yar Mohammed. With the addition of Sind and the Punjab to the Indian dominions (in 1843 and 1849 respectively) the independence of Herat seemed for the moment less important, as India now had a "natural" frontier to the north-west. With this in mind, Lord Palmerston wrote to the British Minister in Teheran in 1851, when the Shah again threatened Herat: "You will, therefore, still endeavour to dissuade the

Persian Government from advancing on Herat, and you may truly say that such a move would not be viewed with indifference by HM's Govt.; but you will be careful not to make any specific threat which HM's Govt. might not be disposed afterwards to carry into execution."[36]

Herat began to sink below the level of imperial consciousness again. The buildings set up by the British Mission crumbled away, the public works were neglected, and all the subsidy money had been spent. When in 1845, a Frenchman, General Ferrier,[37] late of the Persian army, arrived in Herat on one side of a camel (his servant was in a basket on the other side), no European had been seen in the city for four years and excitement ran high – were the golden days of the subsidies to return again? Yar Mohammed was sure that General Ferrier was an Englishman with a secret mission. He was watched day and night, flattered and feasted, then threatened and imprisoned, finally released to continue his journey.

Ferrier found that Herat had suffered greatly from the siege of 1838. The area of the city was at this time about a mile square, surrounded by a ditch and an enormous earthwork crowned by the famous walls. Over the north end of the city towered the citadel, a square building made of burnt brick complete with moat and a drawbridge which was taken up at sunset every night.

Within this medieval city lived about 20,000 people, less than one third of the population which had lived there before 1838. Ruins were everywhere – only one house in five was occupied or habitable. The four long covered streets described by Conolly in 1830 were still standing when Ferrier came to Herat, and there were shops down both sides of the streets, which led from the east, west and south gates, and from the citadel to the market place in the centre of the city. They were tolerably straight, and from twelve to sixteen feet wide. The four quarters of the city were criss-crossed with numerous crooked and narrow lanes, the largest not more than twelve feet wide, and some only six or seven feet wide. Some of these lanes too were arched over, and further houses had been actually built over the arches. So the city was not only confused horizontally, but also vertically.

The houses were generally built in the form of hollow squares, with all openings facing on to the interior square. They were usually two and three stories high, with very thick brick and mud walls, and vaulted roofs of similar materials. The larger houses had stables and servants' quarters attached to them, and all houses were surrounded by their own parapet walls.

The city had several caravanserais, with large courtyards where travellers might stay. There were also many reservoirs, some capable of containing many thousand gallons of water. All these were filled, however, by an aqueduct leading into the city from the hills, and as part of the aqueduct had broken down, a hollow pine tree was used to bring the water across the city's moat.

The great mound of earth which surrounded the city was its principal defence, together with the wall on top of it, and was sufficient to withstand any light artillery guns which might be brought against Herat. But something very peculiar was happening to the mound: the inhabitants, like moles, were digging away at its foundations and the wall itself was in danger. Houses were built against the mound, the slope being dug out to enable house walls to be built, and from the houses small rooms were occasionally excavated from the mound itself. The leveller parts of the mound were covered with graves, and horizontal diggings were frequently made in the steeper parts to provide further graves. In many places the wall itself and the ramparts could only be reached with great difficulty, over the roofs of the houses and between the graves, by men in single file.[38]

Inside the crumbling wall Ferrier found the ruined city. "Buildings of all kinds, caravanserais, bazaars, baths, &c. were nearly all destroyed by the Persian shells or fell to the earth from being abandoned by their owners. The besieged also pulled down many of those nearest to the walls to repair the breaches made by the enemy's guns. Nothing can be imagined more desolate than the appearance of the city in 1845; the traces of the wanton destruction of gardens and houses in the environs, originally so picturesque and fertile, was still apparent; villages and handsome esplanades, shaded by beautiful trees, have completely disappeared. The Persian troops during the ten months' siege, one of the most memorable in the annals of Eastern history, made greater havoc and devastation than if the country had been a prey to civil wars for a hundred years."[39] Even the tombstones had been used by the invading Persians as cannon balls.

The people of Herat Ferrier found to be living in medieval superstition and ignorance. The "doctors" had inherited medicines from the British Mission but had forgotten their application or had never known it – they gave the drugs in ever increasing doses until they had some (or other) effect. One had not been very successful with a bottle of cynate of mercury – he had given it to 100 patients but only one of them had been "cured", the other ninety-nine had died.

Some of the Heratis spent all their days trying, like

Chaucer's alchemist, to turn iron into gold: they believed that all European gold coins were base metal transformed by a magic formula. They could not believe (and who can blame them) the Frenchman's earnest explanation that it was due solely to European principles of political economy, order and justice that European nations owned so much gold.

General Ferrier also noticed that the Heratis depended on astrologers' forecasts for the conduct of their lives. Some days were lucky, some were not, and on unlucky days one stayed put. Conolly had seen with amazement soldiers returning from a campaign waiting outside Herat because the astrologers predicted that an auspicious hour for entering the city would not occur for *four days*. Ferrier too was not taken to see the Vizier of Herat until the omens were favourable.

In spite of their poverty, ignorance and superstition the people of Herat remained light-hearted, fond of pleasure and fanatically devoted to their famous city. They liked to go every day to the meadows outside the walls, and passed the day there in shooting, racing, singing, joking, dancing, drinking and sleeping. They habitually wore red shirts and red trousers, a cloak and a turban. In winter all classes wore lambskin cloaks embroidered with silk.

Ferrier left Herat to continue his journey to India, and it was thirteen years before any other Europeans came to Herat. Yar Mohammed, of whom a contemporary wrote: "if there was an abler or a worse man in Central Asia, I have not yet heard his name"[40] (and the competition was considerable), died on 10th June, 1851, of natural causes, the sole ruler of Herat to do so for many years. He died at Meerilla, a place some distance from Herat, and when the news of his death reached the city the greatest confusion prevailed, all the shops closed immediately and rioting and looting followed. By degrees some order was restored, and Yar Mohammed's son and heir, Mohammed Khan, went to live at the citadel.[41]

In 1852, the Persian army again attacked Herat, this time successfully, and formally annexed Herat as part of the Persian empire. The British representative in Teheran, having failed to persuade the Shah to abandon his claims to Herat, urged the British Government to send a force to attack the Persian Gulf. As a result of the threat, although the British expedition was not sent, the Shah signed an agreement with the British representative in 1853, promising to give up Herat, which subsequently he did.[42]

Shah Mohammed Khan had survived the Persian invasion. He was feeble and perhaps even half-witted: but he managed to keep his precarious hold on the throne for four years until he was in rapid Central Asian fashion besieged, betrayed, dethroned and murdered by Mohammed Yusuf, nephew of that Prince Kamran from whom Yar Mohammed had taken away all power. The legitimist line was thus re-established in 1855 in the person of this Mohammed Yusuf, who was a member of the family which had formerly ruled both Kabul and Kandahar, but which was now separated from the rulers of Afghanistan by a blood feud. The "King Maker", the man who helped Mohammed Yusuf the throne, was one Esan Khan.*

Mohammed Yusuf's accession was not greeted with pleasure in either Teheran or Kabul. Because he was an

* Little is known of the 1853 attack on Herat and Shah Mohammed Khan's rule, because no European observers were at Herat during this period.

Afghan the Persians wished to overthrow him: because his uncle Kamran had arranged for the one-time ruler of Kabul to be hacked to pieces in 1818 there could be no alliance with Dost Mohammed Khan, the dominant man in Afghanistan. The government of India, about to conclude an alliance with Dost Mohammed, was being carefully neutral in the face of strong pressure from the Dost who wished the Government of India to encourage him to capture Herat for himself.

Into this delicate situation a diplomatic brick was dropped by the head of the British Mission in Teheran, one Charles Augustus Murray, who was just about to leave Teheran after quarrelling with the Persian government. Murray, on his own initiative, sent a message of congratulation to Mohammed Yusuf on his accession – thus annoying at one blow the Government of India, the Government of Persia and the *de facto* Government of Afghanistan. Lord Dalhousie, the Governor-General of India, was furious and wrote: "We cannot watch the Persian at Herat, because the Minister has left the Shah's court. We cannot do what would be pleasing to Dost Mahomed because the orders & acts of the Home Govt. fetter us to silence – and while we are sufficiently displeasing him by silence on this side, our minister at Tehran, before he goes, finds time to offend the Dost mortally by quite unnecessarily congratulating the Dost's enemy on his success! Wah Wah!"[43]

The Heratis watched their new ruler making overtures to Murray, Persia and Kabul, and did not like what they saw. The "King Maker" Esan Khan was particularly anxious, for as a pro-Afghan he was likely to lose his head if the Persians took Herat. But with both Persia and Kabul planning an attack on Herat an alliance must be made with one or the other: so that Esan Khan applied to the Afghans for help, but Mohammed Yusuf called in the Persian army.

The Persians moved first, and Mohammed Yusuf soon regretted his dependence upon them. A Persian army arrived, but instead of waiting a seemly distance from Herat began to menace the city. One of the Shah's officers tried to seize the citadel of Herat by a trick, and when this failed the Persians besieged and took nearby Ghorian. Mohammed Yusuf, finding like the Sorcerer's Apprentice that he had conjured up more than he could handle, then appealed for British help to the nearest responsible British officer, Colonel John Jacob of Sind, announcing theatrically that he had hoisted the British flag over Herat, and would stand beneath the flag until rescue came from the British.[44]

John Jacob, who received this remarkable message, was one of the legendary frontiersmen of his time, creator of Sind and founder of Jacobabad. Fierce, independent, incredibly efficient, he ruled his land with a rod of iron. He modelled himself on Cromwell and his soldiers were to be Ironsides. He had an impediment in his speech which perhaps made him uneasy in company, and he was too much in a hurry to be tactful, so that he was always in trouble with his nominal superiors. His voluminous letters were scrawled so fast that they were very difficult to read, and the sand thrown on the ink by his impatient hand still gleams on page after page. He was used to messages from Central Asian princes in temporary difficulties, and when he received the message from Mohammed Yusuf, without referring the question to his superiors, he wrote back expressing British indifference to the whole question, and assured Mohammed Yusuf that the Government of India had no intention of interfering. This reply seriously embarrassed both the Governments of India and Great Britain, and brought upon Jacob a massive rebuke from Calcutta and Bombay, for the governments were already considering war with Persia.[45] To ensure the independence of Herat was one reason. Another was to extricate the honour of Charles Augustus Murray, envoy and Minister plenipotentiary to the Court of Persia.

CHAPTER TWO

Murray in Teheran

IN 1854, Lord Clarendon appointed the Hon. Charles Augustus Murray as British envoy and Minister plenipotentiary to the Court of Persia. It was an unlucky appointment for both Britain and Murray, and Murray was afterwards to remember bitterly how little he had wanted to go to Persia at all. The Foreign Secretary had no time for Murray's doubts however, and he "seemed vexed" and in a thicket of pronouns observed that "as her Majesty's Government had paid him the compliment of appointing him because they thought him the fittest man to be sent on the occasion, he considered it his duty to accept it."[1]

Charles Murray was the second son of the fifth Earl of Dunmore. His mother was the daughter of the Duke of Hamilton and his godfather a royal prince. His childhood was spent between London, Tunbridge Wells and Scotland, as his parents followed the geographical movements of the Season. He was educated conventionally at Eton and by a private tutor.

In 1823 he went up to Oriel College, Oxford, where his tutor was John Henry Newman (afterwards Cardinal Newman). The two men were a complete contrast – on the one hand the gentle scholarly don who was to set the Church of England by the ears, but still, in 1823, unknown outside his small circle – on the other hand the fashionable dissolute undergraduate, holding noisy parties in his rooms and playing stupid practical jokes. Murray thought little of Newman, "he never inspired me, or my fellow-undergraduates, with any interest, much less respect: on the contrary, we disliked, or rather distrusted, him . . . He always struck me as the most pusillanimous of men – wanting in the knowledge of human nature; and I am always surprised, and indeed never can understand, how it was he became such a great man."[2] What Newman thought of Murray is not recorded.

One of Murray's escapades was a ride from Oxford to London and back in a day, to win a bet. He and Lord Edward Thynne won their bet, but one of Thynne's horses died from the effects of the race. His biographer hints darkly at other "less creditable" episodes. Murray made a large collection of (stolen) bell-pulls and door-knockers whilst at Oxford, including a large bell which had belonged to Newman. In between times Murray played tennis, and won a silver racquet, of which he later wrote: "This is the only incontestable distinction that I can claim to have achieved in my long life."[3]

Before he was twenty-one, Murray formed an ambition to become a Fellow of All Souls, then a very different kind of institution from that of to-day. It was not one of those places stigmatised by Murray as "reading colleges", quite the reverse, and the Fellows were known as "Bene nati, bene vestiti, moderate docti". There were no objections to Murray becoming a Fellow except that he was under age, but he claimed his privilege as son of a peer, and was elected. He had however, no particular subject, no particular interest, and though he remained a Fellow of All Souls for some years "it is difficult to discern . . . any definite purpose for the disposal of his life, either on the part of Charles Murray himself or of his parents."[4]

Still a Fellow of All Souls, Murray set off to see the world. He went round Europe and across the United States. In America he met and fell in love with Elise Wadsworth, daughter of a rich American landowner. Mr Wadsworth refused to allow the two to marry as Murray's parents would not hear of him settling in the United States and Wadsworth would not allow his daughter to live in England. To stay in America, Murray tried to become Secretary of the Legation in Washington, and though he was not successful, the diplomatic service was eventually to become his career.

On returning to England, Murray stood for Parliament three times without success, until Lord Melbourne took pity on him and found him a place at Court, where according to Murray's own account, he used to help the young Queen with bad advice in games of chess and draughts.

After seven years with the queen, Murray's diplomatic career began at Naples, and continued at Cairo, where he won the name of "Hippopotamus Murray", not because of his diplomacy, but because he introduced into Europe the first hippopotamus to be seen there for fifteen hundred years. In their old ages, Murray and his hippopotamus would meet frequently in Regent's Park, Murray shouting greetings in Arabic and the animal lumbering up with what were alleged to be welcoming rumbles.

By 1850, Murray was tired of Cairo and hoping for employment elsewhere. He had disagreed with his chief at Constantinople, Sir Stratford Canning, in such violent terms that he expected to be removed without promotion or even employment. His reputation as Egyptian consul would rest on his two great achievements, the building of the railway to join Alexandria to Cairo* and ultimately to Suez, and his famous animal.[5]

In 1850, Murray returned to Scotland, there to meet again by chance Elise Wadsworth, with whom he had fallen in love fourteen years before in America. They married, but less than a year later, she died giving birth to a son. Murray was given the consulship at Berne, leaving his child to be brought up by a relation. Soon, however, he was writing to Lord Dalhousie, the Governor-General of India, "The Fates (represented by Lord Clarendon) have again turned my face towards the East; by the next post you will see me gazetted as Minister in *Persia*: – it has not been without a struggle that I made up my mind to go so far away from my only & motherless child, but I thought that at a crisis like the present [the Crimean War] when so many are called upon to sacrifice their domestic ties and feelings, I should not be justified in declining to accept an appointment which recent events have rendered more than usually important."[6] Three years later Murray was to write: "The past cannot be recalled: if it could, I should try to recall *many* acts of folly that I have committed, and among them all perhaps the greatest, the having allowed myself to be persuaded to come out to this nest of intrigue, falsehood and villany comprehended in the word Persia."[7]

Murray's journey to Persia was prolonged because the ordinary route by Trebizond and Erzeroum was in the hands of the Russians. As he neared Teheran, he grew more and more depressed, and on his arrival affairs were worse than his worst fears. The Mission House was crumbling: the paper falling off the walls, the curtains in rags, the chairs, tables and sofas repaired twenty times and literally falling

* The first railway in Africa, opened in 1854.

to pieces, and not a single cupboard in the house. The Foreign Office had authorised a total expenditure of £200 to refurbish the embassy, which might possibly have covered the cost of bringing furniture to Teheran but which certainly would not have actually bought anything.[8]

In Murray's view the state of the Mission House was the fault of the Foreign Office. For years the Mission had been organised from Calcutta, and he thought it was a great pity that the transfer had been made from the Government of India to that of Whitehall. He complained that the Foreign Office, unused to the way business was conducted in the East, and apprehensive of House of Commons questions, thought only of economy. They had reduced the salary of the envoy, taken away the travelling and table allowances, removed the bodyguard, and worst of all, abolished the customary presents which sweetened the formalities of Eastern courts.[9] Word came to Teheran before Murray arrived that he was bringing an offensive and defensive treaty against Russia, and a few million tomans for the expenses of the war, so that when the Shah and his chief minister, the Sadr Azim, found that Murray brought no presents and had neither a treaty nor a loan in his pocket, their disappointment knew no bounds.[10]

The Russian envoy on the other hand, not hampered by an economical Foreign Office, lived in a splendid house in Teheran, surrounded by a glittering retinue and bodyguard, and gave elaborate presents to the Shah and his chief ministers. Murray was bound by his masters in England to offer friendship and little else to Persia, whereas the Russian, not noticeably hampered by the British passion for truth, offered rich subsidies and wide provinces as the reward of alliance with the Czar.[11] It was to counteract the Russian influence in Persia that the British Mission and a similar French Mission had been sent to Teheran at all. The alliance of British, French and Turkish in the Crimean War was not being very successful, and were the Persians to join the Russians, the situation might have become much worse. It was therefore important that the British and French envoys at Teheran worked together to outshine the Russian: but this was not easy.

The Shah had taken a great dislike to Murray and his Mission before ever he saw him. This was partly because Murray had spent a long time at Cairo, and was a great friend of the Pasha of Egypt and the Imam of Muscat, both enemies of the Shah. The Persians thought it odd that this friend of their enemies should be sent to Teheran.[12] Another reason for the Mission's unpopularity was the advance publicity given to it: *The Times* especially had a wide circulation in the East, where the opinions of the paper were taken to be those of the British government.* On Murray's departure for Persia, *The Times* had a paragraph to the effect that Murray "*would soon bring his Majesty's nose to the grindstone.*" Some busybody found this and translated it to the Shah. "Conceive the effect," wrote Murray, "of such a phrase upon a Monarch who has been a spoilt child from infancy & has never heard himself styled otherwise than 'Centre of the Universe' 'King of Kings' etc. etc. etc."[13]

The first minister, Mirza Aga Khan, whose title was the Sadr Azim, was at this time the real governing power in Persia. He was between forty-five and fifty, with a long face, a long Persian cap above and a long flowing black beard

* *The Times* was circulated inside the besieged city of Sebastopol, where the Russians could read in Mr. W. H. Russell's despatches of the besiegers' plans and disposition of troops.

below. He was grave and dignified in public, but jolly in private and apt to tell indecent stories, of which he had a great store. His energy was prodigious, he worked all day and most of the night, for he wanted to see and know everything that was going on, and he overlooked every department of government. Always surrounded by secretaries, he gave out orders, had them written in his presence, sealed them, and sent off the couriers himself. As well as all his government business he also ran personally a merchant's business (and made a fortune) selling rice, silk, salt, etc. He had many enemies and was much criticised, but he substituted a gentler rule for the savageness of his predecessors, and while he was in power there were few atrocities. He had a great fondness for his relations (or perhaps found them more trustworthy than others) and tended to promote them all to some kind of office.[14] He was also adept at all kinds of deception, truth was not important to him, and he made rings round Charles Murray. He was obviously, from everything he did at this period, a very clever man, and one has the feeling that he enjoyed his tightrope diplomacy in Teheran, those years of the Crimean War. He had three envoys to juggle with, and two of them, the Russian and the British, could and would put an army into Persia if they thought she was on the other side. The British might attack from the south: the Russians could bring pressure to bear on the whole northern frontier. Considering the proximity of the Russians and the state of the war the Sadr Azim quoted: "a hyena at hand is more to be feared than a lion afar," smiled on the Russians, cold-shouldered Murray the no-present man, and amused himself by flirting with the French.[15] The Sadr Azim and Monsieur Bourée, the French envoy, constantly visited each other and exchanged presents, decorations and compliments. This infuriated Murray, for instead of supporting Murray in his frequent disputes with the Sadr Azim, Bourée continually urged the Englishman to be more conciliatory, to make concessions, not to be so prickly.[16]

The second man in M. Bourée's Mission was an aristocratic Frenchman called Count Joseph Arthur de Gobineau, whose terrible claim to fame is to be the theorist whose ideas of the supremacy of the Aryan race influenced Wagner, Nietzsche and the Nazis. He came eagerly to Persia in 1855, to see the cradle of the Aryan race where all his theories would be justified – and found to his indignation that racial prejudice was almost non-existent and that even negroes were treated as equals . . .[17]

*

When Murray arrived in Teheran there had already been trouble over a "Mirza" or Persian secretary, called Hashim Khan. The trouble, which had been allowed to smoulder quietly in the time of the last envoy, was fanned by Murray into an enormous bonfire, with widespread repercussions.

Hashim Khan was brought up as a page in the household of the previous Shah.[18] He became one of the Shah's confidential bodyguards and eventually an officer in the regular army; he married a woman of doubtful reputation, who had had two other husbands, but her chief claim to fame was that she was the sister of the Shah's principal wife.

One Persian summer, when the Shah and his court were as usual encamped in summer quarters, Hashim Khan applied to the prime minister for an increase in salary. This was refused, and the minister told him that he would not give him any more money, and that he might go about his business. According to Murray, who later heard a version of the interview from the Sadr Azim, he added "and get more money where you can." Hashim Khan thereupon applied to the British Mission, and was at once (in 1854) appointed First Persian Secretary to the Mission.

To the Persians this appointment was undignified, because of Hashim Khan's own aristocratic background and because of his wife's relationship to the Shah. Moreover he had never officially left the employment of the Persian Government. These obstacles might have been overcome, but the Sadr Azim had a long-standing feud with Hashim Khan's family, and disliked him personally: he immediately protested at his appointment to an important post in the organisation of the powerful British. Hashim Khan was not free to work for the British, because he was only a deserter from the army who had taken sanctuary in the British embassy. No documents in his writing would be received by the Persian Government. Obviously the Mirza's usefulness in Teheran as a Native Secretary in these circumstances would be strictly limited, and Thomson, the head of the Mission, climbed down, turned Hashim Khan out of the First Secretary's tent in the camp, and appointed another man. But as the Sadr Azim would not promise to leave Hashim Khan alone, he was allowed to remain in the safety of the Mission precinct, with no official post and no pay – presumably doing unofficial work for the British and being fed by them.

Murray found Hashim Khan sheltering in the Mission still, more than a year later. Something must be done with the man, who was well qualified and could be trusted not to betray British interests to his enemy the Sadr Azim. Murray decided to appoint him as British Agent to, of all places,

Shiraz, a town of strategic importance and doubtful loyalty in the west of Persia, far beyond the effective control of the Persian Government. This appointment, which seems to have been made in all innocence by Murray, and was supported by the Foreign Office, was violently opposed by the Persian Government throughout the quarrel. The Sadr Azim threatened that if the Mirza left his sanctuary for Shiraz he would instantly be arrested and any disturbance blamed on the British.

Murray wrote threatening letters to the Sadr Azim about diplomatic immunity, the Sadr Azim wrote back threatening Hashim Khan should he put his nose outside the Mission gates. Suddenly all over Teheran, in the palace and the bazaars, gossip gathered round the name of Hashim Khan's wife, the dissolute princess. Her visits to the Mission House had been too frequent, and her name was coupled with that of Thomson, the last envoy, and that of Murray himself. The Persian Government tried to warn the British minister, but taking no notice Murray allowed Hashim Khan to bring his wife to the summer quarters of the British Mission at Gollahek and place her in a tent among those belonging to the Mission, only separated by a single wall. This was sufficient proof for the Persians: an innocent woman, or even a discreet one, would have lived in the village a hundred yards away from the camp.

On 14th November, 1855, the princess was seized by her outraged brother and imprisoned in his house. She was threatened with forcible divorce* unless she and her husband set up a respectable household once more. Murray, playing straight into the hands of the Persians, sent the

* A Moslem husband could obtain a divorce by saying "I divorce you, I divorce you, I divorce you".

Mirza to demand his wife's release, which was refused. Murray then wrote to the Sadr Azim who replied, on Saturday, 17th November, that he could not possibly discuss the affair, as it touched on ladies, and moreover on royal ladies, and even worse on the honour of His Majesty. He would decently pretend that Murray's letter had never reached him.

Goaded to action Murray replied that the matter must be discussed, or on Monday, 19th November, at twelve noon, he would haul down his flag and break off diplomatic relations with the Teheran Government.

The Mission settled down for the rest of the weekend: Sunday was a day when Victorian diplomats did not do business. On Monday morning, just before noon, the Sadr Azim acted and sent a messenger to Murray asking for a delay of two hours to allow him to consult the Shah. This was followed by a further two hours' delay because the Shah had only just returned from hunting. Just before sunset the Mirza went to demand his wife and was refused. All was now set for the final breach, Murray was about to give the order to strike the flag – when the Ottoman Chargé d'Affaires came in, and begged a further delay. About 10 p.m. Murray received notes from both the Ottoman Chargé d'Affaires and the French ambassador, asking for a further delay of some days, this time because the Shah had departed to visit his mother. Murray refused, and made up his mind to act. But it was now after sunset, and the Mission flag had already been lowered for the night: the effectiveness of hauling down the flag was lost for another day. On Tuesday morning it came down, and the Mission prepared to leave Persia.

Murray did not go quietly. He had been trapped and like

a beast in a trap he snarled at everyone. Especially he blamed the French ambassador, who had, he thought, never behaved well. When Murray asked the Frenchman to travel to Persia with him at the outset of the Mission, the Frenchman preferred to arrive in a French warship. After that the Frenchman had continued to employ in his Mission the son of the First Interpreter of the Russian Minister, although France and Britain were at war with Russia and although Murray pointed out to him continually the error of his ways. Altogether the Frenchman was too friendly with the Russians (he was also having an affair with Comte de Gobineau's wife). The Russians were studying the original documents of the Murray-Sadr Azim correspondence when the French ambassador asked to see them; for this too Murray blamed the Frenchman, though it is not clear why. M. Bourée believed the scandal about Murray and the princess to be true.* "But," wrote Murray indignantly, "the Mirza's wife is old, ugly, and married to her 3rd husband."[19]

There was rioting in Teheran over Murray and the princess – there had been a serious riot some years earlier (in 1829) over two Georgian girls who had been detained in the Mission House of the Russian diplomat Greybayedoff. The Russian envoy and almost all his suite, casual visitors to the Mission, and even the girls who were supposed to be being rescued had been killed by the mob.[20] In spite of the danger in which he stood, Murray's demands grew higher and higher as the final negotiations crescendoed. He at first wanted a formal visit by the Sadr Azim which all Teheran

* Napoleon III made a remark to this effect to the British ambassador in Paris. Was Murray guilty? He never admitted it, but his contemporaries seem to have accepted that he was: and M. Bourée had no political reason for wanting Murray to be in disgrace, rather the reverse.

would notice, with the return of the Mirza's wife to her husband's house near the walls of the Mission. As the correspondence grew more and more offensive on both sides he wanted more and more. The recognition of the Mirza as in British employ, an apology and recantation by the mullahs of Teheran for their endorsement of the slander: later, after leaving Teheran, Murray wanted the humiliation of all Persia and the dismissal of the Sadr Azim from office. He wrote to the Governor-General of India: "if Lord Palmerston & you do not make the Persian Government 'howl for this' there is no faith in man."[21]

It was more than a fortnight before Murray was ready to leave Teheran on his "agreeable little promenade of 800 or 1,000 miles on horseback in midwinter."[22] As he made his way out through the Bazaar surrounded by the members of his Mission and followed by 100 heavy mule-loads of tents and other baggage, he saw the soldiers waiting to seize Hashim Khan – but forewarned, he had been ordered to stay in the Mission House. Murray withdrew to Tabriz, but by the time he arrived the winter had already set in with great severity, and the snow had fallen in such quantities in Kurdistan and Armenia that it was dangerous for caravans to go farther. Month after month went by as he waited for revenge on Persia, to be dealt out by the British Government (under Lord Palmerston) or the Indian Government (now under Lord Canning).

CHAPTER THREE

Dost Mohammed Khan at Kabul

WHILST Murray was waiting in the mountains for his revenge on the Persians, they were advancing on the city of Herat. Colonel Jacob's discouraging reply to the Heratis' appeal for help almost caused the city to be surrendered, but the rulers of Herat still thought there was a chance that aid might come from Dost Mohammed Khan, the chief power in Afghanistan and Emir of Kabul.

This remarkable man was then at the height of his power. The Kashmiri biographer of Dost Mohammed recorded that at the time of his father's death (he was murdered) he left twenty-one sons and "several" daughters by his eight wives. Dost Mohammed was the twentieth son, and thought little of by his half-brothers, because his mother was of humble birth and of a Persian tribe.[1] At the time of his father's death the whole clan of brothers, the Barakzai, was in danger of extinction at the hands of the Sadozai ruler of Kabul. But their fortunes changed and one of Dost Mohammed's brothers, Futteh Khan, became firstly minister and then ruler of Kabul. Dost Mohammed Khan gradually became more and more important to his brother. He was always loyal, always polite to his over-bearing half-brothers, always obedient to their orders even when they included political assassinations. When he was twelve he became Futteh Khan's water-bearer. After some time he was also allowed to prepare his brother's smoking pipe.[2] From such humble beginnings he rose to be the most trusted commander of Futteh Khan; he remained a wild young man, living the life of a dissolute soldier, and was often seen so drunk that he could hardly stay on his horse.

Like Shakespeare's Henry V, he "emerged out of a cloudy morn of vice," a graceful handsome boy, to become supreme in Kabul after his brother's murder. Having achieved power he reformed himself completely, taught himself to read and write, gave up drink and bent his considerable ability to the business of ruling. He was always accessible to his subjects, and like a medieval king listened to their complaints and dealt out justice as he rode through the streets. "Is Dost Mohammed dead that there is no justice?" became a proverb. He was "beloved by all classes of his subjects . . . he administers justice with a firm and steady hand . . . Idolised by his troops, he is perhaps the only prince in these countries who regards the quality rather than the quantity of his men."[3] He was cunning and politic as well as brave, and only employed the sword as a last resort. He was greatly wronged by the British in India, but once he had come to terms with them kept his side of the bargain with great resolution.

The Dost's appearance was to the traveller Masson, not imposing – among his gaudily-dressed chiefs his plain white linen would hardly be noticed.[4] He was about five feet ten inches high, thin and sinewy. There is a portrait of him drawn about 1836 by an Englishman – his face looks proud, clever, is dominated by a high wide forehead and a large eagle nose.[5] He had a great passion for horses, and every day he was in Kabul in the hot season he would ride out to the garden of Timour Shah on the edge of the city to see his horses. There he would sit on a special platform, sheltered from the sun by aspen and mulberry trees, while around him were picketed perhaps 300 horses, his favourites being nearest.[6]

In 1836, after ten years of power, Dost Mohammed wrote a polite letter to the newly arrived Governor-General of India, Lord Auckland. "The field of my hopes, which had before been chilled by the cold blast of wintry times, has by the happy tidings of your Lordship's arrival become the envy of the garden of paradise." He concluded: "I hope, that your Lordship will consider me and my country as your own."[7] He little thought how this oriental compliment would be taken – two years later Auckland gave away Dost Mohammed's country to another man. Auckland and his advisers, plotting at Simla, had decided that the Dost's friendliness with the Russian envoy at Kabul endangered the security of India, particularly as the Persians, who also favoured the Russians at this time, were at the gates of Herat. If Herat fell, and Afghanistan became pro-Russian, it might have just been possible for the Russians to move via Herat to the North-West Frontier. So with great foolishness Auckland ordered an expeditionary force to be prepared in India to march across the Indus, by a roundabout route and through some of the worst country in the world, to raise the siege of Herat and to replace Dost Mohammed by a former Emir, Shah Shujah, who had lived in exile in India for twenty-two years.

There was no moral justification for this war, which was called by Colonel Jacob "foolish and wicked", which failed in all its objects and ended in the worst military disaster in the history of British India. The siege of Herat, which had been defended with the help of Pottinger, was raised before ever the expeditionary force set out, when a British force reached the Persian Gulf: there was then less reason for the Afghan war than ever. But once the wheels were turning, no one liked to halt, and the former Emir was duly restored with considerable difficulty to his not very loving subjects. For a time Shah Shujah was kept on the throne in Kabul by a large army of occupation, but mistake after mistake was made by the British political officers, and in December, 1841, the British envoy Macnaghten was murdered by Dost Mohammed's son. Incredibly the 4,500 British and native troops capitulated. In the depths of the Afghan winter the beaten army with 12,000 camp followers, women and children, began to retreat to India. A week later a sentry on the ramparts of Jalalabad, the nearest fort held by the British, saw a solitary white-faced horseman struggling along the road from Kabul. It was Dr Brydon, "the Remnants of an Army,"* the only man of the entire army to reach safety, for the rest lay dead on the passes and in the valleys behind him. Only a handful of hostages were saved from the slaughter, one being Eldred Pottinger who had been caught up into the Afghan war.[8]

The British sent another expedition to punish Kabul, but this time after marching up the country and down again they withdrew completely from Afghan soil. Dost Mohammed who had been kept in honourable exile in India returned to his city, and was thereafter left in possession by the British. For his part he had been greatly impressed by all he had seen at Calcutta, and was heard to say that if he had formerly understood the military resources of the British he would not have opposed them.[9] In 1854 (when Murray was travelling to take charge of the Mission at

* The title of a famous painting by Lady Elizabeth Butler of Dr Brydon's arrival at Jalalabad: in the Tate Gallery, London.

Teheran), the Emir asked for a treaty with the East India Company, which was finally concluded at Peshawar in March, 1855.[10] By 1856 he had just seized power at Kandahar, and was more anxious than ever to add Herat, once the third region of Afghanistan, to his dominions.

When he received an appeal for help from Herat, Dost Mohammed immediately suggested to the Government of India that he should be helped with Indian money and arms to repel the Persians. At this point (May, 1856), the government was bound by orders from London not to offer any advice or aid to the Emir,[11] and the Governor-General, now Lord Canning, was obliged to reply to the Dost that he could not give him any help.

However, when it was realised in London that Herat was about to fall to the Persians the authorities changed their policy quickly: and wrote to Canning directing him to assist Dost Mohammed and to give him muskets, money and British officers.[12] They changed their policy quickly – but it had taken two months for them to reply to Canning and it took five weeks for their new instructions to reach Canning, being carried overland to Marseilles, through the Mediterranean by sea, overland from Alexandria to the Red Sea, and by ship from the Red Sea to Calcutta.[13]

By September, 1856, Herat was still being defended against the Persians but by Esan Khan. Mohammed Yusuf had been caught plotting to surrender the city to the Persians, and had been sent ignominiously into the Persian camp, from where he was sent a prisoner to Teheran. As Mohammed Yusuf had done months before, Esan Khan now in his turn appealed to the British, sending messengers to the Chief Commissioner of the Punjab. He offered the city of Herat and its dependencies to the British government, accompanying the offer by the strongest protestations of fidelity and devotion to the Government of India. He asked for British troops or at least one British officer (all the rulers of Herat were bewitched by the memory of Eldred Pottinger) and mentioned as an afterthought that he had found the treasury empty. Canning refused him men, because of the difficulty of protecting them, "the heavy train of consequences which would follow if we should have the blood of British officers to avenge, make me entirely opposed to the risk of so great a stake for a very uncertain advantage,"[14] but he sent a message to the waiting envoys offering money, about £30,000.

But it was already too late. A few days afterwards, before any money could reach Herat, Esan Khan in his turn made a pact with the Persians. On 25th October, the Persians entered the city, and Esan Khan was retained as governor with a Persian garrison in the citadel.[15]

*

Herat fell on 25th October, but Dost Mohammed Khan and the Government of India's representative had not yet met to discuss aid to the Afghans to defend Herat. The news of the capture of the city took nearly a month to reach India, for it was not until 21st November, that the Chief Commissioner of the Punjab, Sir John Lawrence (afterwards Governor-General), telegraphed the news to Calcutta and asked for instructions. Even the telegraph took two days to reach Canning. He immediately followed the customary course of sending the message round the members of the Council, in order of seniority, each member scrawling his views on the original message and then sending the paper on. The completed messages look like the left-overs of a game of consequences and it is amusing to see the characters of the writers revealed by their notes.

Canning wrote on the docket that he believed a subsidy and officers should be offered to the Dost in spite of the fall of Herat. The senior member of Council wrote (typically): "I agree: the event however is most unfortunate." The other three members added their views, and a Council meeting was held three days later to draft instructions to the Chief Commissioner of the Punjab. The Dost was to be offered money to equip his army, and "should the Ameer ask whether we are disposed to support him in possession of Herat, you may answer that we shall not interfere with his possession of it – our object is that it should not be in the hands of Persia. Be certain – to wait for this question to be asked – which will be an excuse for acting contrary to Home Instructions."[16]

*

At the end of the year of 1856, the Dost Mohammed Khan came to the Afghan end of the Khyber Pass to negotiate with the British. Fearing treachery he asked that the British negotiators (Sir John Lawrence and Herbert Edwardes) meet him on Afghan soil. On 1st January, 1857, two of the Dost's sons and a party of wild horsemen appeared in the British camp to escort Lawrence's party up the Khyber Pass – the first time that any of the Englishmen there had seen the inside of the pass, surely the most romantic in the world.

John Lawrence, who also feared treachery, had left orders that if firing was heard within the pass his troops should at once enter it and attack. This order might well have cost the lives of the whole party, for when they reached

The Hon. C. A. Murray and his staff: (*l.* to *r.*) a servant, Murray (seated), Major R. L. Taylor (confidential secretary), the Mission doctor, the Mirza

Dost Mohammed Khan, Emir of Kabul

Lord Canning, Governor-General of India 1856–1862

Commander Richard Ethersey, Indian Navy, Commodore of the Persian Gulf Squadron (*l.* mounted) and Captain Felix Jones, Indian Navy, British Resident in the Persian Gulf (*centre* mounted) at the Residency, Bushire

The Persian Expedition

the Afghan camp, a salute was fired by the heavy guns in front of the Emir's tent, a salvo taken up by the muskets of the Afghans who lined the lower hills and by the mountaineers who crowned the tops for miles along the pass, until the whole of the Khyber rang and rang again with the echoes. Fortunately the commander of the British troops outside the pass decided that the firing could only be a salute and did not therefore rush to the rescue.[17]

Dost Mohammed Khan rode back to the British camp for the talks. He appeared to the British to be very old (he was about 70), he had a long white beard and rode an elephant, being unable to cope with a horse.[18] His early death was expected by all, especially his numerous sons, who were only waiting for him to die to fight over his kingdom. His treasury was empty, and his army starving. Nevertheless he was to live until 1863, and before he died saw all Afghanistan in his power.

He came in to Jamrud in British territory, passing through a line of 7,000 British troops, a mile long, drawn up to do him honour. It took almost the whole of January for an agreement to be reached between the Dost and Lawrence. What the Dost thought of Lawrence is unrecorded, but Lawrence thought the old man untrustworthy: "I confess that I felt no confidence in anything which he said. His interests at present lead him to turn to us. But there can be no security that he will remain faithful one day longer than seems convenient. He has no sense of shame. He sent me as a present, the only one he made, ten horses and two mules, nearly all of which were spavined and worn out. The whole lot did not fetch 1,000 rupees [£100], and this notwithstanding the princely way in which we treated him!"[19]

In spite of his parsimony in the matter of presents, Dost

Mohammed was as clever as he was impressive and an excellent story-teller. He would sit up all night, telling the most amusing stories to Lawrence. He was fond of talking of his poverty, and explained to Lawrence that every year he had to borrow from the money-lenders who were usually Persians. "They know that as soon as I am dead my sons will spring at each other's throats, that there will be general anarchy, and that they will lose everything. So when they press me for payment I call them together and, putting on a long face, tell them that I am being killed by anxiety about money. They see it is better to forgive the debt, and keep themselves and me in life and prosperity a little longer. And so we all start afresh."[20]

On 26th January, at 4 p.m., the agreement was signed in Lawrence's tent. Canning had been consulted by telegraph* and he had authorised the terms. As he described them "the result is that after a patient hearing of the old man, who vapoured a good deal at times about blowing up walls and carrying everything within them at the point of the sword, it appeared certain that nothing commensurate with the cost, was to be expected from arming the Afghans against Herat. Their requisitions were, the raising of the Afghan army to about 50,000 men, an increase of its Artillery to 100 guns (they have now about 60), and an expenditure on our side of at least 65 lacs a year [about £650,000] . . . This larger scheme therefore was dismissed . . . The question of frontier defence then came under considera-

* The telegraph was introduced into India by Lord Dalhousie in 1853, and by 1857 there were 4,555 miles of telegraph lines in the country. But there was no telegraph link with England until 1870, and at the time of the Persian war it took two to three months for the government of India to send a letter to England and receive the reply.

tion . . . and the chief provisions are that the Ameer shall keep up a certain force – 18,000 infantry besides his present Cavalry and Artillery . . . and the Govt. of India shall pay to him one lac a month."[21] British officers were to be sent in an advisory capacity, and 4,000 more muskets were to be supplied to the Afghans, in addition to the several thousand muskets and five lacs of rupees already sent.

In the event the arms and men were not used against Herat, but nevertheless the agreement was satisfactory to both sides, and the subsidy was quietly continued throughout the Indian Mutiny. Lawrence turned out to be wrong about the trustworthiness of the Dost Mohammed Khan, for he kept his side of the treaty for the rest of his life, and stayed above the North-West Frontier in peace while the Mutiny was threatening the whole system of British government in India.

CHAPTER FOUR

India prepares for war

LORD CANNING and his wife had landed at Bombay on 28th January 1856, at sunset, to see for the first time the vast land he was to govern with so much success. That great and good man Charles John Canning (2nd Viscount and 1st Earl Canning) was as yet undistinguished, the quiet son of the statesman George Canning. In his youth he had worried his mother by his indolence, his vagueness, and his rather endearing fault of owning a yacht but refusing to own a house.[1] On his marriage to Charlotte Stuart, daughter of Lord Stuart de Rothesay, he did buy a house (and kept the yacht) and applied himself to politics, becoming first Commissioner for Woods and Forests and then Postmaster-General (to Rowland Hill, he was the best Postmaster-General he ever had). But when he was made Governor-General of India – at a salary of £25,000 with houses and servants provided[2] – he had not made any great mark on public affairs.

The India which Canning saw in 1856 was a great hotch-potch of races, languages and forms of government. There were the British dependencies, the half-dependent states who were aided by the British and the wholly independent states. States in the second and third categories had been moving into the first category rather too fast for the administration to cope with, and this is one reason why Canning and not a more aggressive man was appointed to

India: he was to consolidate the *status quo*, and not to acquire new territories. Eleven days after he landed at Bombay and nominally in the Governor-Generalship of his predecessor Lord Dalhousie, a new province, Oudh, was annexed to the Government of India. "I have received orders to do Oude,"[3] wrote Dalhousie and after the annexation: "So our gracious Queen has 5,000,000 more subjects and £1,300,000 more revenue than she had yesterday."[4] Oudh was to prove very nearly too much for the British; but Persia was the principal problem Dalhousie handed to Canning on the new Governor-General's installation in March, 1856.

In 1856, British India was still nominally ruled from Leadenhall Street in the City of London, the offices of the East India Company, John Company. In practice the cuckoo had grown so much too large for its foster-parents that the British Government was obliged to interfere from time to time. The British Government directed Indian affairs through the Board of Control, headed by a president, whose appointment was political and who had a seat in the Cabinet. The Board could override the Company's ruling power, which was the Court of Directors. For many facets of Indian administration a system of dual control was in force: for instance, the Queen's soldiers were lent to India, where there were then two kinds of regiment, the Company's regiments and H.M.'s regiments. The navy was the Company's, but the Royal Navy helped police the coast and supplied some of the highest ranking officers.

Foreign affairs were also run under a dual control; the British envoy in Persia represented both the Government of India and the Government of Great Britain. When Canning found himself involved with Persian affairs, he received instructions from both Downing Street and Leadenhall Street on his conduct.

The Government of Great Britain intended to keep Persia independent: but even more important was the protection of Herat. The province was to remain neutral, a buffer state between Persia and Afghanistan, to protect the North-West Frontier. Canning's instructions were to remain on the most friendly terms with the rulers of Afghanistan, but to avoid interference with their dynastic problems. He was to recognise *de facto* rulers and not to enter into any discussions about rights.[5] If the Persians captured Herat it would become the duty of the government in England to decide what measures should be taken to maintain the independence of Herat as an important element in the defence of British India against the probable machinations of Russia.

Before Canning had even reached India it looked as if the troubles with Persia might lead to war. There was the business of Charles Murray and the withdrawal of his Mission from Teheran. Murray was demanding action from the governments to avenge the insults he had suffered, and as early as January, 1856, the Cabinet was debating whether or not to send gunboats to the Persian Gulf.[6] But the members of the Cabinet were not all of one mind, and by April Canning was assuring the President of the Board of Control that he would keep the peace until further instructions arrived "unless the Shah should steam up the Hooghly with Murray swinging at his yard-arm."[7]

For most of 1856 the uneasy peace continued,* whilst

* There was an attempt by the Persians to make a treaty with the United States Government which, if effective, would have reduced British influence and harmed British interests in the Persian Gulf. This was regarded by the British as an unfriendly act. The treaty appears to have

possible campaigns were debated in London and India. Canning was appalled at the thought of fighting Persia at all. He wrote "I contemplate the prospect of the inglorious and costly operations which lie before us with more disgust than I can express."[8] To him "all wars are noxious, especially to India which can't raise the money to pay for them."[9] However, if Herat had to be saved, it must be done either directly, by an army sent through Afghanistan, or indirectly, by attacking Persia in the west, as had been done before, until she retreated in the east.

With Dost Mohammed Khan ruling in Kabul, it is not surprising that Lord Canning did not want to risk sending an army through Afghanistan. He wrote: "I believe it to be impossible for an English army to show itself in that country without at once alienating the common herd of the people, who do not care a straw for Herat, but who have a lively recollection of 1838 and all that followed."[10] Subsequent Afghan history was to prove him right. There were other reasons besides the obvious dangers. Canning believed that a united Afghanistan, friendly to the British, would prove a better barrier to Russian advances on the North-West Frontier than any garrison in Herat. "I don't believe that one Indian official in a hundred who talks of a campaign in Afghanistan has really given thought to the nature of the people of that country, and to the means and mode of dealing by which we can best enlist them on our side . . . Help them liberally whenever they stand in need of help for honest purposes – punish their marauding tribes on the frontier sharply, and above all quickly – encourage no

---

been stillborn. (India Office Library MSS. Eur.F.75, Elphinstone to Jacob, 15th July, 1856.)

family feuds, and eschew the *divide et impera* doctrine – do your kindnesses with as little show of interference as possible – and, especially, be always better than your word with them."[11]

Persia was much more easily attacked from the Persian Gulf, where the maritime provinces lay. On the coast, too, there was more scope for future operations than at Herat, for Herat lay alone, the only place of importance in a large area. It would not be the first time that the British had attacked Persia from the Gulf, and conditions on the coast were well known to the Government of India: the state of the country and of the Persian army were equally well-known, because for many years British and European officers had helped to train Persian troops.

The shores of the Persian Gulf were, and are, a desolate region. Before the exploitation of the oil along the coast, there was little to attract anyone to the Gulf. The British were interested in the control of the seas, partly to safeguard the route of their telegraph lines to India and partly to suppress the slavers who brought negroes out of Central Africa up through the Gulf. At sea life in the Gulf was almost tolerable; on land it was extremely difficult. Supplies and water were always short. The climate was deadly to Europeans at certain seasons, and even to the Turks – out of a Turkish garrison of 350 at the north end of the Gulf in the summer of 1853, 200 died of fever.[12] Towns and villages were very few. There was no fuel. The few inhabitants had nothing to sell or barter. There were no local draught animals for hire, there were no artisans, no boats, few roads, no tools. If the tribes were hostile they would destroy what little they owned, rather than trade with the enemy; but as the tribes were in a state of chronic revolt against the

Teheran Government it was more likely that they would join an invader, particularly if the invader was winning. But this was equally undesirable, because of the "innate propensities of all tribes there, to indulge in plunder and rapine, rather than pursue legitimate trade."[13]

The possible points of attack in the Gulf were the island of Karrack, Mohammerah at the head of the Gulf, Bushire and Bunder Abbas on the eastern shore. The first was in favour with the Cabinet in January, 1856, when Granville wrote to his friend Canning ". . . Murray's letters to the Shah are singularly offensive. His demands are quite absurd; yet orders are to be sent to occupy the island whose name I forget in the Persian Sea."[14] It was soon evident however, that the occupation of Karrack alone would not achieve much, for in August Canning wrote: "the Persians abandoned it some weeks ago, upon the approach of one or two innocent steamers, with an alacrity which did not look as if they set much store by it."[15] The climate of Mohammerah (now called Khoramshahr) was deadly to Europeans between May and October, and could not be continually occupied. Bunder Abbas was leased to the Imam of Muscat, a friendly ally of Britain. Bushire therefore was considered the most suitable target: it was the chief sea port, and provided a safe anchorage, but was easily defensible on the landward side. Much of the trade of that province of Persia depended upon Bushire, and to save it the Shah might withdraw from Herat and even reinstate Murray.

So Bushire was decided upon as the first target in the projected campaign. Charles Murray, writing from exile in Baghdad, at this point suddenly produced a trump-card of his own, a name which has become very famous in the twentieth century, but which was almost unknown in the

1850s. It was that of the first Aga Khan, great-grandfather of the present Aga Khan. After an unsuccessful rising against the Shah, he had fled from Persia and was in 1856 living in Bombay as a pensioner of the Bombay Government, but as the head of the sect of Khojahs and son-in-law of the late Shah he could command a great following in Persia. At least so Murray thought. His plans for the war were "Bushire will presumably be blockaded or bombarded, and the Aga Khan let loose upon his own country, with one or two thousand men to help him at first until his adherents join him."[16] Nothing was ever done about the latter half of this plan however, and the Aga Khan lived peacefully in Bombay until his death.

Into the Gulf, to Bushire, a force might be sent by the Indian Government. What kind of opposition was it likely to meet with there?

In 1855, a report was sent to the Foreign Office on the Persian army.[17] So pitiable was the state of the army that the writer of the memorandum concluded that it would be safer to fight against the Persians than alongside them – whoever allied with the Persians would have to begin by giving the soldiers their back pay for many months. The nominal strength of the army was 86,700, but of these only 20,000 were considered fit for duty. There was an artillery force of 6- and 12-pounders, but the ammunition for the guns had to be carried on the backs of camels or mules, as there were no ammunition carts. Many of the artillerymen were completely untrained. The regular cavalry were only 500 in number, trained by an Austrian officer: great numbers of irregular cavalry – about 150,000 – could be dangerous in a guerrilla war, but like the feudal levy they resembled would not stay in arms for long.

Officers and men of all ranks lived at home, attending to their own domestic, commercial and agricultural affairs, being called out by the provincial governors when there was military work to be done. Only the regiments doing duty in Teheran received any training.

When he was called out for active service the Persian soldier was entitled to one year's pay, which was 7 tomans (64s.) and 1d. per day in lieu of rations. But of the 7 tomans only 2 actually reached the soldier, the rest being taken by the officers or the regimental accountants. It was quite common also for part of the 2 tomans to be paid in spoilt wheat. Even this was usually in arrears. Discipline in the army was savage. When the soldiers were at war, there were no pensions to their dependents, or allowances: there was no medical department at all, sick and wounded soldiers were left untreated. Under such conditions, the soldiers usually suffered in silence, but would evade duty if the prospect of remaining unpunished were good. When off duty the underpaid soldier would take a menial job such as street porter or bricklayer to keep his family from starvation.

The arms of the soldiers were as defective as their pay. Many of their muskets were unusable, without bayonets or with defective locks. Within regiments, and even within companies, there were muskets of different calibres and models, using different types of ammunition, so that it was very difficult to distribute ammunition to the men. The better muskets in the army were outdated British ones.

The Persian army on campaign was greatly hindered by the great numbers of camp followers which trailed it everywhere – this was a problem for all Eastern armies, including the Indian army. Every one or two soldiers had an ass or a horse to carry their very limited equipment. Every officer had an entourage of horses, mules or camels to carry an unnecessarily large quantity of useless kit, so that an army of only 2,000 infantry was accompanied by about 12,000 animals for the officers *alone*. Food for so great a number of animals was only obtained with difficulty, and the soldiers were too busy providing for their animals to have much time for military duties.

In May, 1856, nineteen battalions of the Persian army were near Herat, a quarter of the whole army. Some troops were in Teheran and some on the Russian frontier, leaving only eight battalions in the whole province of Fars (in which Bushire lay), an effective strength of 5,000 men. There was no Persian naval force at all in the Gulf.

*

Lord Canning had a very much more effective force to use. Although the Indian army, especially that in Bengal, was already full of the weakness which led to the Mutiny of 1857, and although the officer corps and indeed the European part of the army generally was dangerously undermanned, there was no doubt that the army was a formidable weapon.

Each of the three Presidencies of British India (Bengal, Bombay and Madras) had its own army. There were three types of regiment: firstly European regiments (three in each Presidency) of European soldiers with European officers, secondly and greatly in the majority regiments of native infantry (sepoys) with native and European N.C.O.s and European officers, and thirdly irregular cavalry of native troops with a small number of European officers. These made up the Company's army. There were also some

British regiments of the Queen's army always in India (the regiments served in rotation) hired by the East India Company from the Crown (about twenty-six of these in 1856).

The history of the Indian navy, as told by its historian, C. R. Low, is a sad tale of inefficiency and neglect. It was always so small that many officers who had passed their promotion exams had no posts – there were none vacant. Often government economies (the navy was financially under the control of a military board) brought salary cuts, and abolition of posts. Comparatively the sailors were worse off than the soldiers, and the navy was always subordinate to the Royal Navy. Promotion was by seniority only, and merit was not of the slightest importance.

The sailors were native seamen as well as Europeans, and as late as 1830 a commander was found guilty of piracy for taking thirty negro boys from the coast of Africa as "marine boys".[18] Conditions below decks were terrible for both officers and men; "the Service had ever been remarkable for the devotion to duty of its officers, who, from time immemorial, went uncomplainingly to the worst climates of the world, in the worst of all possible sailing craft human ingenuity has devised, the ten-gun brig or 'coffin', and the still smaller schooner, which were less than five feet in height in the 'tween-decks."[19] Even these ships were usually second-hand. In 1839, the *Kilkenny* was added to the service, a vessel which had formerly carried pigs between Waterford and Bristol. She was renamed the *Zenobia* but was nevertheless a great failure in the Indian navy.

The least popular station of the Indian navy was the Persian Gulf. It was very unhealthy and many officers died –

during the years 1826–50, four commodores, eleven lieutenants, two pursers and fifteen midshipmen died in the squadron and no less than four-fifths of the survivors had to go on sick leave. In the days before the Persian war there was no regular mail from Bombay to the Gulf, and only when a cruiser arrived to relieve another, or a casual sailing ship (for a merchant steamer was never seen) dropped anchor in Bushire was there any news of the outside world or mail from England. There were newspapers, but they were six or nine months old before they reached Bushire. The squadron felt totally cut off. There were some recreations, hunting the gazelle, cricket matches, seine netting, hawking and pig shooting. Even at Bahrein there was swimming, in a beautifully clear deep freshwater pool. But sometimes the Gulf squadron was near despair: "it was this utter expatriation, more than the detestable climate and the discomfort and confinement on board a miserable little brig or sloop-of-war . . . and when the only resource was an exchange from the intolerable heat of Bushire Roads, where the ship lay three miles off the town . . . to the even hotter pearl banks of Bahrein, it is only surprising that more officers did not betake themselves to the last resource of despairing humanity, drink, or suicide."[20]

*

As soon as Lord Canning took office as Governor-General the preparations for war with Persia had begun – in fact even earlier the Bombay Government had had instructions to prepare a force. Everything had to be taken to the Gulf, from hospitals (15 detached bungalows) to horse-shoe nails. Smiths and carpenters were as vital as artillerymen. Fodder had to be sent for the animals, and vegetable seeds were taken to provide future food.[21] From March to September the preparations went quietly forward.

Indian waters in 1856 were seeing the change from sailing ships to steam. For the expedition to the Gulf as many steamships as possible were to be used, and additional sailing ships would be towed by the steamers – a very slow and somewhat dangerous proceeding. Nine steamers of the Indian navy received sailing orders for Bombay and the Gulf and twenty-three transports were chartered, while three steamers of the P. & O. Company and three steamers of the Bombay Steam Navigation Company were to be requisitioned – at the last minute for reasons of security.[22]

This fleet was to transport 6,000 men from the Bombay Presidency, including two European regiments (H.M.'s 64th Regiment, later the Staffordshire Regiment, and the 2nd Bombay Europeans who subsequently became part of the Durham Light Infantry). The fleet sailed in the end with 5,670 soldiers, of whom 2,270 were Europeans, with in addition 3,750 camp followers, 1,150 horses and 430 bullocks.[23]

Once the preparations for war had begun, they seemed to gather momentum of their own accord. It was 1855 when "that ass Murray" left Teheran: it was January, 1856, when the Bombay Government was asked to prepare for war, March, 1856, when Herat asked for help, September when instructions for war were sent by the East India Company, October when Herat fell, November when the expedition finally left for the Persian Gulf. Originally intended to punish the Persians for their treatment of Murray,[24] the expedition became also an "imperial war" to protect the North-West Frontier, without apparently any policy decision in London or Calcutta. "What are we to do?"

wrote Canning plaintively in 1856, "I hope the Instructions will tell us – or at least that the object and scope of the war, if we are to go to war, will be duly defined by the Govt. at Home."[25]

The command of the expedition to the Persian Gulf in 1856, was given to Major-General Foster Stalker, in his 58th year, one of the most distinguished officers in the Bombay army. A shipbroker's son, Stalker had spent all his adult life in the Company's army since he joined as a cadet in 1818. He had been the first commander of the 2nd Bombay European Light Infantry (which became eventually part of the Durham Light Infantry) when the regiment was raised in the 1840s. At the time of the Persian expedition he was described by one of his junior officers as "a nice old fellow, not valiant in Society, but they say very sturdy and sensible."[26] A darker side to Stalker's life was that, like many Indian officers of his time, he was always in money difficulties. He had hoped to be clear of debt and to be able to retire, but shortly before the expedition sailed he had stood as surety to a brother officer who failed to pay the debt – Stalker was left with yet another heavy financial burden.[27] He was not a brilliant soldier but seemed to be reliable – in the whole of the Bombay army there was no officer who had commanded a large force in the field, and the Governor of Bombay wrote sadly that at the top of the army tree there was little more than dead wood. The Governor-General and the Governor decided rather reluctantly that Stalker "might do".[28]

The naval commander of the fleet was originally to be Captain Richard Ethersey of the Indian navy, known in the Service as "Grim Dick".[29] As a lieutenant he had commanded a ship in the China war of 1840–2 and had been recommended for a C.B. (then awarded for gallantry) which he did not get, however, because of a rule which prevented naval officers of lower rank than captain holding the decoration. He commanded the Indus Flotilla until 1855 when he was sent to command the Persian Gulf squadron. The first Ethersey knew of this 1855 appointment was the announcement in the newspapers – he was bitterly angry because the squadron only consisted of a sloop, a brig and a schooner, and he was sent only because the C.-inC. of the Indian Navy disliked him and wished to do a favour to the officer who was supposed to take command of the squadron[30].

Ethersey was, however, a good man to command the expedition's naval force because he was able, popular and knew the coasts of the Gulf well. But he was superseded, a very unpopular move, by the C.-in-C. who so much disliked him. "Admiral Sir Henry Leeke, Commander-in-Chief of the Indian Navy – a purely administrative appointment – has been authorized to take command, in defiance of an order from the Court of Directors, not six years old, to the effect that the naval Commander-in-Chief should never hoist his flag beyond the port or quit sight of headquarters, unless in cases of extreme emergency. The gallant Admiral, now in his 70th year, has never hitherto sailed, save as a passenger, in the Eastern waters, and of the climate, hydrography, and peculiarities of the Persian Gulf he must needs be as ignorant as he is of the native character and tongue . . . He supersedes Commodore Ethersey, one of the ablest and most experienced officers of the Indian navy."[31]

Sir Henry Leeke was very lucky indeed to be still in the service in 1856. He was an officer of the Royal Navy, one of the many of post rank who applied for the job of C.-in-C.

of the Indian Navy, with its salary of over £3,000 a year and a house allowance. In 1848 he had very nearly been made C.-in-C., but the casting vote of the Chairman of the Court of Directors of the East India Company, Sir James Lushington, gave the post to a relative, Captain Stephen Lushington.[32] Nevertheless Lushington resigned in 1851 and Leeke was then elected. "It was many years since he had commanded a ship at sea, and his service afloat had been uneventful; he was neither distinguished as a sailor or administrator, and, for the rest, was an amiable, kind-hearted gentleman, not more unfitted for his post than most men possessing these virtues as their chief recommendations to high command."[33] Since he had come to India (four months after he was appointed) he had been in a lot of trouble. He was reprimanded by the Government of India in 1852, 1854 and in 1855. In 1855 he was involved in the case of the *Assaye*. The officers of the *Assaye* had insulted some Arab chiefs visiting the ship at Aden and Sir Henry, who was personally involved, made himself President of the Court inquiring into the incident[34]. The Governor-General Lord Dalhousie subsequently wrote of one of Sir Henry's circulars about the case that it "is the most irregular, injudicious and objectionable document I have ever seen proceed from an officer of his rank . . . I know this officer of old & his professional character. The Govt. at home wd. never have entrusted him with such a command and we suffer for our sins in having him imposed upon us."[35] But nothing was done. And when Canning arrived, fresh from England, in 1856, Leeke applied for the command of the naval force as if it was his right and was appointed before Canning was warned against him.

One of those who became involved in the Persian War

at a humbler level was Lord Canning's nephew and Military Secretary, Lord Dunkellin, son of the Marquis of Clanricarde. His military career (he was in the Coldstream Guards) had begun in the Crimean War – "This remarkable young nobleman distinguished himself, in a signal manner, in the Crimean campaign, by blundering, one evening, among the trenches, and getting himself peaceably taken prisoner, with much ease and safety. But the late Emperor Nicholas, either disdaining to keep captive such a small deer, or being really desirous to propitiate the British aristocracy, straightway returned Dunkellin to his disconsolate parent, without exchange or consideration . . . Lord Dunkellin is doubtless a great blessing to the paternal roof, but Lord Clanricarde, with a stern Roman virtue, despatches him beyond seas again with all convenient speed. He is sent out to Calcutta, on the staff of his uncle-in-law, the new Governor-General, Lord Canning. And the hero of the Crimea loses no time in distinguishing himself again, and in such a way as makes it probable that he will be again handed back, with despatch, to the paternal embrace."[36]

On 14th June, 1856, Dunkellin arrived in Calcutta. His post as Military Secretary was a personal appointment, mainly concerned with military patronage and organising the A.D.C.s. He was a great delight to his aunt, who was bored by the inactivity expected of the Governor-General's lady, and lonely because of the grandeur of her position which so intimidated visitors that no one would speak to her or even stand near her if they could avoid it. Dunkellin arrived "prosperous & merry & bearded & red"[37] full of gossip which he retailed to Lady Canning all day, even at breakfast.

Dunkellin however, was soon very bored in Calcutta, and wrote in September: "This is far away the dullest stupidest place I ever was in in my life, and I do not think I can stand it long . . . The women here with very very few exceptions are not pretty, and are continually in the family way . . . if once I get home he will be a sharp fellow who catches me here again except as a future G[overnor]-G[eneral] & I don't think *that* likely. Horses are bad & dear – the general run of cuisine beastly, the wine third rate if so high. I am getting bald." What happened to enliven Calcutta is described by Dunkellin in a letter to his friend Gregory:—

They got up a ball, a *public charity ball*, for the benefit of the inundated French, and put me on the Committee rather against my will. Two or three days before the ball I was asked if I would give a ticket to a Kept Woman who was to go there with her *married* sister, and *her* husband, who I was given to understand was a clerk in some office. It being a public ball and for a charity I never thought twice about it, but gave the tickets, only stipulating that the parties were to be decently dressed and properly behaved. Well the ball came off and a slower duller and better behaved one I never saw. I must tell you that I never had anything to with either of these women and only knew one by sight and from having addressed her twice, the other not even by sight, nor did I know she was "gay". However at the ball some fool twigged them, and one young ass instead of being quiet took out the kept party to dance. The parties who twigged them did nothing for three or four days, and then out burst a storm of virtuous indignation principally I believe from people who were not there, but who wrote anonymous and pungent letters to the papers, who I think most indecently took it up, and abused me like a pickpocket . . . Of course when the papers opened the whole thing was stirred up and I was positively alarmed at reading that I was an intimate friend of the women, was perpetually at their house, had boasted of my intention of forcing *them* (they added a third to the number) into Calcutta Society, and a swarm of things I had never dreamed of.[38]

The Bishop of Calcutta denounced Dunkellin from the pulpit[39] and Canning, despite the indignant cries of his relatives, forced Dunkellin to make a public apology. This Dunkellin did in such a way as to infuriate the Anglo-Indian press even more, and he was given leave of absence for an indefinite period. He left Calcutta, and went off to visit his friend, Charles Augustus Murray, now licking his wounds in Baghdad; but on the way Dunkellin found himself involved in the Anglo-Persian War. Lady Canning sent Dunkellin for the war a medicine chest and a book entitled *It's never too late to mend.*

Lord Dunkellin found himself involved in the Persian War by accident, but most of the European officers in India were very anxious to serve in the war – they would have in wartime a chance for promotion, glory and prize money which could establish them for life. Acting-Lieutenant F. W. Brown of the 20th Bombay Native Infantry borrowed £100 from his father to buy a new tent and to pay "some very pressing debts" before setting off eagerly with his regiment to join the sailing ship *Result.*[40] One of those moving heaven and earth to go on the expedition was the newly-arrived Cornet Charles Combe of the 3rd Bombay Light Cavalry, who had landed in India a day after Lord and Lady Canning. He was soon well-settled in at Rajkote, in a "bungalow" of his own, a better than usual bungalow for a subaltern because it had an upstairs room. For this he paid £42 a year unfurnished. He employed a married butler at 30s. a month and a boy at 16s.

a month. As soon as he arrived he had "begun drill, which is rather hard work; five o'clock in the morning is the time I get up, and after a cup of tea, I ride down to drill, which lasts till about 7.30; at 12, I have an hour more carbine, &c. drill, and in the afternoon have another hour and a half foot drill. We dine at mess at seven, and generally get to bed at about ten."[41]

There were rumours of war with Persia in the regiment as soon as Combe arrived, and in mid-September the 3rd were told that they were to be part of the Persian expedition – all except the unlucky cornets who were additions to the strength of the regiment. Combe and his fellows were "frantic at the idea of not going with the regiment, and are trying everybody who has any influence at Head Quarters. The weather gets very hot again, but nobody thinks of that, or anything but 'service in Persia.' "[42] The regiment was preparing for war, the swords were all sharpened and the steel scabbards lined with pieces of wood.

On 1st October, 1856, the 3rd left Rajkote in heavy rain, amidst the tears and lamentations of the soldiers' wives and relatives. On the eve of departure the cornets received permission to go with their regiment after all, to their great delight. That first day the regiment only marched six miles towards their port of embarkation, yet the night was a complete fiasco, as the ground was so wet that the horses' picketing pegs would not hold, nor could the tents be properly pitched. The men had to stand by their horses all night, yet many got loose and kicked and fought, and in the morning two had to be shot and many were severely injured. It took nearly a fortnight to march to the sea, but it was never again as bad as that first night. Combe enjoyed the journey, and wrote home: "This is a very jolly life, we march about two a.m., halt about seven, have two hours 'stables', after which tents are pitched, and breakfast prepared, stables again in the evening, dine at six, and 'to bed' very soon afterwards in the small tents; the large ones and baggage going on to the next stage about nine o'clock."[43]

While Cornet Combe was preparing for the campaign, a strange situation arose at Bushire. The governments of two countries had decided to go to war, but the British Resident in the Persian Gulf who lived at Bushire, Captain Felix Jones of the Indian Navy, had had no news for seven weeks and did not know if it was to be war or peace. About this time a ridiculous incident happened. A steamer was sent to Bushire by the Government of India, with a despatch box supposed to contain an important despatch, a sort of ultimatum for the Shah of Persia. But on arrival when the box was formally opened, it was empty, and the steamer had to return to Bombay to find the despatch. Someone thought that someone else had put it in, and between them all, the important despatch on which the question of peace or war mainly rested was lying quietly in some office in Bombay.[44] All that Captain Jones knew was that the steamers from the Gulf were withdrawn to India and he was left stranded. If he and other British subjects were suddenly ordered to leave the country, they would have no means of so doing.[45]

But Captain Jones was to see another British ship before the war began. On 27th September, the Company's steamer *Feroze* dropped anchor in Bushire Roads. In the Resident's absence (he was away at a country house), the *Feroze* disembarked two Commissariat officers and an officer of the Quartermaster General's department with their baggage and retinue, who began calmly to collect information about supplies for the proposed army of invasion. It was like the Constantinople Force of 1915 trying to buy maps of the Gallipoli Peninsula in Cairo bazaars before the expedition sailed for Gallipoli. The *Feroze* also brought into Bushire the ordinary mail from India to Bushire, containing, of course, many references to the expedition's preparations at Bombay.[46] The Persians might not have a very good army but they were not stupid – Jones returned to Bushire to find that the whole town was in an uproar, the merchants were panicking and the civil and military authorities of the countryside beginning to collect troops.[47] The gentlemen from the *Feroze* were rushed back on board again and the ship sailed for Bassadore, leaving Jones to sweat it out alone for nine more weeks, until December when the *Hugh Lindsay* at last sailed into Bushire with orders to take him off.[48] Long before, on Thursday, 13th November, the last transport of the invading fleet had weighed anchor in Bombay harbour and set off across the Arabian Sea for Bushire.[49]

CHAPTER FIVE

The Persian War – Bushire

WAR was declared on Persia just before the fleet sailed, on 1st November 1856. The official declaration of war dwelt on the siege of Herat in breach of the agreement of 1853 between the Persians and the British as the cause of the expedition – no mention was made of Mr. Murray.[1] The Government of Bombay issued a flurry of notices about the war, and in the rush one notice passed the Governor unread. It was an official government notice, a General Order, thanking the officers who had taken part in organising the expedition, and by an oversight the notice gave precise information about the entire force, detailing the regiments, the number of troops, horses, armaments, etc. It was a mistake, wrote the Governor of Bombay anxiously to Lord Canning, but he supposed that the Persians already knew the strength of the army.[2]

In Persia the news of the *Feroze*'s arrival at Bushire with the landing of the commissariat officers had caused panic in the bazaars of Teheran. The Shah, Nasir-u-Din, ordered the priests to proclaim a Jiddah, a holy war against the infidels,[3] and hoped to rouse not only his own subjects but also the Moslems of India.

The Persian Empire had centuries before been the mightiest in the world, but had long since lost all but the memory of those days. Now Persia was crumbling as the Russians and Turks and Afghans made fresh encroachments on

Persian territory. The Persian people themselves were divided between Arabs, Turks, Kurds and Leks (the original Persians), and so strong was the Turkish influence that even the royal family spoke Turkish for choice and Persian only on ceremonial court occasions.[4] The Shah took little interest in government and left everything to the Sadr Azim, who was busy feathering his nest, building palaces, collecting and burying treasures, and promoting his relations. Meanwhile commerce was decaying, all public works halted and every branch of revenue and administration disorganised. The state of the country reminded a European traveller of feudal Europe – for instance, sanctuary in shrines was still in operation throughout Persia.[5] The priests declared the law, but civil officers of the state administered it, thus doubling the opportunities for corruption. Many of the people spent their whole lives indebted to the money-lenders, whose interest was limited legally to twelve per cent, but in reality seldom amounted to less than twenty-five per cent and often to fifty per cent or even 100 per cent; "the entire nation seems to be in debt, commencing with the Shah, who is in debt to the Emperor of Russia, and ending with the humblest muleteer."[6] Tax collection and an iniquitous system of free provisioning of travelling officials led to further oppression of the people. Slavery still flourished, although the slaves were not treated with contempt as in America. There was no unifying force amongst the different tribal units, and a Persian proverb marks their independence of authority: "I and my tribe against the nation. I and my cousins against the tribe. I and my brothers against my cousins. I against my brothers."[7]

The Persians struggled to survive these hardships, and their burdens of a "corrupt Court, incapable and timid

Ministers, impoverished resources, a divided people, and provincial governors in whom no dependence can be placed",[8] but their numbers were dwindling, and many of the towns seemed to a European traveller of the 1850s to be half empty. For instance, in Tabriz "Half the city seemed depopulated; there were large spaces wholly vacant, with deep excavations on either hand, from which the earth had been dug to build houses. Dead dogs, and here and there a dead horse half eaten, offended more than one sense. The houses were frightful. Constructed of brown unburnt bricks, looking exactly like mud, and without a single window to the street, they presented a most gloomy aspect. This is a general picture of a Persian town; and be it remembered that Tabreez is one of the best and richest cities in the whole kingdom."[9] Some of this depopulation seems to have been due to lack of irrigation water – the government was too inefficient to keep the channels in working order.

*

Nevertheless, to a generation brought up on tales of Haroun-al-Raschid and the Arabian Nights, Persia seemed a very romantic place, and the military expedition to Persia set out with high hopes. Lord Dunkellin dreamed of military glory and of Persian houris, "their eyes, shapes & heaven."[10] General Stalker, Admiral Leeke and Lord Dunkellin were all in the same ship, oddly enough the *Assaye* which Leeke knew only too well. Rough weather in the Arabian Sea troubled the soldiers, and Dunkellin was reported to be remarkably quiet. The General was not entirely free from seasickness, "the chaplain in an awful state, one or two in that sort of way when the cover was taken off the curry, they were obliged to hurry on deck."[11] As the ships sailed up the Persian Gulf, then not famous for oil but only for slave traders, the land appeared much drearier than the soldiers had imagined. High precipitous cliffs, of brownish-grey colour, rose sheer from the water's edge, without any sign of vegetation or human life. Many rocky islands of the same desolate description lined the coast.[12]

The steamships of the expedition reached their destination some days before the sailing ships (the tow-lines were cast off on entering the Gulf), and the first captures of the British Force were the small pearl-fishing islands of Karrack and Kergo, about thirty miles W.N.W. of Bushire, which were surrendered without a shot being fired.[13] Karrack was intended to provide a safe anchorage, a coaling station and a place to put up the prefabricated hospitals brought from India.

From Karrack the expedition moved on its main objective, Bushire. On the morning of Sunday, 7th December, the naval guns opened fire on the date groves of Halilah Bay, a beach about ten miles south of Bushire. As the first shots crashed out, the gunner's mate of the *Ajdaha* remarked to his lieutenant: "There's a dig in the side for Russia, sir."[14]

The guns from the sea met with little opposition and after a few rounds of shells the first soldiers were landed. It was a beautiful sight, Lieutenant Brown wrote to his sister, there were lines of small boats being towed by some bigger boat in front "so they all looked like strings of wild ducks paddling along." Unopposed, the soldiers began to move forward to capture the water wells, vital to their survival. A most extraordinary oversight now became obvious, which was to harass the early days of the expedition. The landing arrangements had been planned on the assumption that it

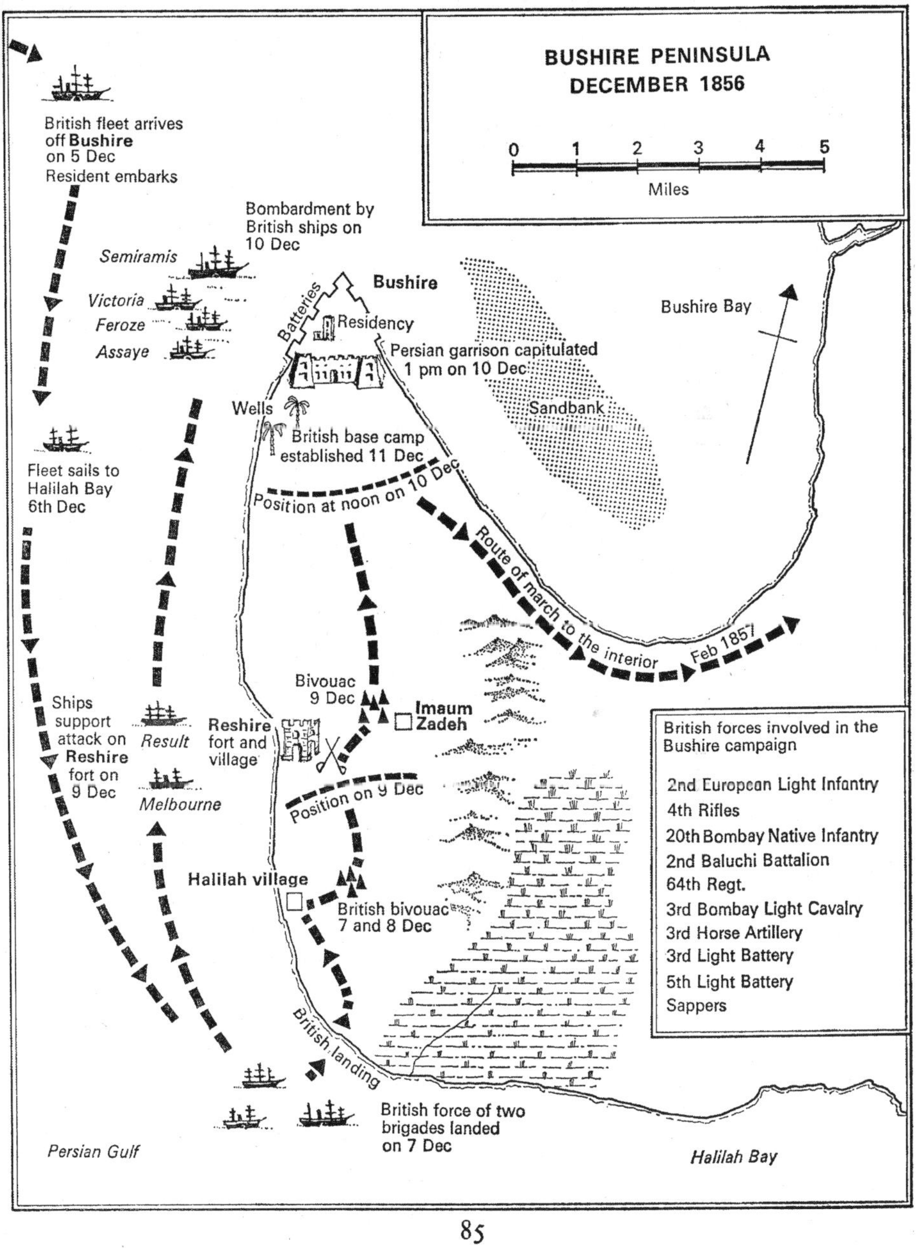

BUSHIRE PENINSULA
DECEMBER 1856
0 1 2 3 4 5
Miles
British fleet arrives off Bushire on 5 Dec Resident embarks
Bombardment by British ships on 10 Dec
Semiramis
Victoria
Feroze
Assaye
Bushire
Batteries
Residency
Persian garrison capitulated 1 pm on 10 Dec
Sandbank
Bushire Bay
Wells
British base camp established 11 Dec
Fleet sails to Halilah Bay 6th Dec
Position at noon on 10 Dec
Route of march to the interior
Feb 1857
Bivouac 9 Dec
Imaum Zadeh
Ships support attack on Reshire fort on 9 Dec
Result
Reshire fort and village
Melbourne
Position on 9 Dec
Halilah village
British bivouac 7 and 8 Dec
British landing
British force of two brigades landed on 7 Dec
Persian Gulf
Halilah Bay
British forces involved in the Bushire campaign
2nd European Light Infantry
4th Rifles
20th Bombay Native Infantry
2nd Baluchi Battalion
64th Regt.
3rd Bombay Light Cavalry
3rd Horse Artillery
3rd Light Battery
5th Light Battery
Sappers

would be possible to obtain both small boats and baggage animals locally, and to the astonishment of the commanders after the shelling of the shore no small boats could be found. The ships' boats had to manage as best they could, and it took two hours to land six guns. Fortunately there was no interference by the Persians.[15] It was later found that there were no suitable baggage animals at all in that part of the Gulf.

Instead of pushing on from the beach towards the town of Bushire, the men now rested for a couple of hours about two miles inland. Then they moved on over a bleak country covered with stones and a rather pleasant smelling shrub towards the high ground above the village of Halilah. When the soldiers came within sight of the village, the headman came running out in a dreadful state of fear, kissed the nose of the General's horse, and went on as if he was crazed. The man's fears were allayed by the interpreter with the force, and soon the villagers were selling supplies to the soldiers, fodder for the cavalry and artillery horses being particularly necessary.

That night of the landing the soldiers bivouacked on the ground, and protected themselves as best they might from the cold and a very heavy dew. They burnt everything they could find and tried to sleep, huddled over their fires, or walked up and down until dawn came. The whole of the next day, Monday, they waited and waited, while the pitiably few ships' boats ferried the rest of the force from ship to shore. Another night was spent on the cold ground, without baggage or shelter.

At 7 a.m. on the morning of Tuesday, the force at last moved. The advance guard of about 350 men and 2 guns marched out towards Bushire, through the sandy ravines between the sea and the 50- to 100-foot cliffs which shut off the coastal plain. There was no incident for about five miles until the village of Imaum Zadeh was reached. This village lay just inland of an old Dutch fort called Reshire,[16] the last defensible place before Bushire itself. From Imaum Zadeh the advance guard of the British force could see that the interior of the fort was full of Persian soldiers.

The walls were nothing but heaped up sand, with a deep dry ditch round the landward side. The ground all round it was broken, covered with loose stones and prickly hedges, and great yawning wells with no parapet round them. The guns were brought up and fired at the fort for a time but it was found quite useless as all the balls stuck harmlessly in the sand: the ships too tried firing, but after killing one of the 2nd Bombay Europeans they thought it as well to stop. The infantry were sent in. "It was dreadful walking," wrote Lieutenant Brown afterwards, "and almost impossible to keep a proper line and presently the bullets began to pitter patter among our ranks."[17]

Another officer wrote that as the enemy opened fire "down went three men at once, and we were hard at it; – ping-ping-whurr-bang – the air seemed to be full of bullets . . . This was the first time I had been under fire, and as I had only my sword with me, I had to wait patiently as a sort of target. I feel truly thankful that I escaped. After the surprise had passed over, I began to wonder what I could do; so, observing a poor wretch crawling along within a dozen yards, I rode up to him, and asked where he was hit? He told me he had a ball in the ankle. So I dismounted, put him on my horse, and took him to the surgeon, who was fully employed behind a wall a few yards further on."[18]

The 20th Bombay Native Infantry, the 2nd Bombay

Europeans and the 64th Regiment stormed the fort of Reshire, each trying to outpace the other, through two old breaches in the walls. The first man on the parapet was Captain J. A. Wood, 20th Native Infantry, who was instantly attacked by a large number of the garrison. These men fired a volley at him at point blank range. He was hit by no less than seven musket balls, but fought on and cut down his chief opponent with his sword.* His men swarmed on to the parapet beside him and after a short, desperate fight inside, no quarter given or asked, the rest of the British force came up and the Persians had had enough. They poured out of the fort close to the sea-shore, and escaped towards Halilah and the hills. Pursuit was quite useless – the horses of the artillery and cavalry were so tired that they could only "walk with a little bit of a trot now and then."

For the third night in succession the tired army spent a very uncomfortable night. No sooner had they lain down on the ground than the alarm was given, and for the rest of the night there was little peace.

In the morning the few British dead were buried. Brigadier Stopford of the 64th had been shot dead on the ramparts of the old Dutch fort, and Colonel Malet of the 3rd Bombay Cavalry was shot in the back by a Persian whose life he had just spared. He had died immediately, only exclaiming, "My poor wife."[19]

The Persians were depressed by their losses at Reshire, which was little more than a skirmish, for the soldiers seemed not to understand the British calling for them to

* Wood survived his injuries and for his part in this action was awarded the Victoria Cross. His regiment, the 20th Bombay Native Infantry, subsequently became the 120th Rajputana Rifles.

surrender, and very many were killed. The Governor of Bushire was blamed for sending a garrison to the ruined fort, equipped with only a few rounds of ammunition for their matchlocks and a few bags of dates for food. It was even suggested that the Governor had thought the garrison expendable, for they were of the tribe of Tungistanis, not pure Persian but half Persian, half Arab.[20]

After the funerals of the expedition's dead and a further rest the force moved on towards Bushire. In advance of the troops Commander Felix Jones, the Resident in the Gulf who had spent such an uncomfortable time in Bushire before being taken off, sailed towards Bushire in a small steamer under a flag of truce. He was to offer terms of surrender to the garrison. But to his annoyance the guns of Bushire fired on him – "I could scarcely account for this conduct, having taken some pains to explain the meaning of a flag of truce, in the event of warfare, before quitting the town."[21] Jones retreated precipitately, but while he was reporting to the admiral, the Persian garrison sent out a messenger under a flag of truce of their own, apologising for firing on the steamer – it was blamed on the ignorance of the artillerymen. Terms were not agreed.

On 10th December, the admiral placed his men-of-war in line of battle, with his flag-ship in the centre. First of all firing at a subsidiary defence south of the town, the ships then moved against Bushire itself, and shelled the walls. So close did they go that every ship ran aground on the falling tide, and for four and a half hours the ships and the Bushire guns cannonaded at each other. The plan of battle had been that the army should attack the south and south-east of Bushire, while gunboats forced the creek to the north-east to cut off any retreat, the fleet bombarding from the sea when the troops were within two miles of the town. But the admiral started his guns firing far too soon, before ever the column had left Reshire, and as the gunboats had not been sent to the creek, many of the Persians escaped out to the north-east, to the hills.[22]

The soldiers, advancing wearily over the hot dusty plain, could hear the tremendous noise of the naval barrage. One by one the Persian batteries fell silent, and a breach was made by the pounding guns in the defensive wall of the town, at the south-west angle. On the approach of General Stalker and the army the Persian flagstaff was taken down, in token of surrender, and at noon the firing ceased.

After surrendering, the governor and garrison of Bushire were for some time reluctant to leave the town, mistrusting the reception they would get; but when a released prisoner was sent in with a note threatening a further assault they gave way. At 4.30 p.m. the British colours were hoisted on what remained of the British Residency: the ships had been ordered not to shell the Residency, but it was subsequently found to be the most heavily damaged building in Bushire. The Governor of Bushire and the C.-in-C. were taken to General Stalker (escorted by Lieutenant Brown), and about 1,500 of the townspeople and irregulars came out of the town to lay down their arms, and stood in front of the British line, about half a mile from the town. As the British colours were hoisted the troops gave a loud cheer – the Persians thought this was the signal for a massacre, and with one accord turned and ran away as hard as they could until they fell exhausted and were recaptured.[23]

The prisoners spent the night sitting in rows on the ground under guard. The were still expecting to be killed, and every time any order was given, or any movement (such as the guard changing) took place, they shouted: "Imaum, Imaum" (Mercy). It was not a peaceful night. It is pleasant to relate that the following morning all those prisoners who had not already escaped (except three senior officers who were to be sent to Bombay) were taken inland by the cavalry and then released. The muskets taken from the prisoners were all found to be stamped with the Tower mark, that is they had been made in England and formerly given to the Persian Government by Britain.

The town of Bushire, now in British hands, contained between seven and eight hundred houses, built of white, soft sandstone, encrusted with sea-shells. The streets between the blind windowless walls of the two-storied buildings were not more than six or seven feet wide, and were everywhere infested with mangy dogs, the scavengers of Eastern towns, and choked with filth thrown from the houses and sand which crumbled from the walls. The houses of the very rich (there were not many of these, about eight) had wind-chimneys rising above the town, sixty to 100 feet high, made so as to catch every breeze and send a current of cold air into the house below. The houses of the poor and the soldiers were merely huts built of date-palm leaves. The population of about 15,000 was an uneasy mixture of Arabs, Turks, Armenians, Persians and Jews.[24]

A Frenchman, landing at Bushire in 1855, had thought the only place in the whole town worth mentioning was the British Residency, which was almost a town in itself, surrounded by its walls with gates guarded by Indian soldiers. The Resident lived in a European-type house, with one story and decorated with columns: his second-in-command had a house, and there were also buildings for the doctor and others attached to the Resident. There were two courtyards, servants' quarters and a large barracks for the Indian soldiers and their officer. Every evening, at sunset, the drums beat the retreat at the foot of the Residency's flag-staff.[25]

News of the capture of Bushire reached Calcutta on Christmas Day[26] and both the General and the Admiral sent enthusiastic despatches about the battles. The Government of India was not so enthusiastic, and the Admiral in particular was much blamed for his refusal to carry out part of the plan of attack, and for failing to provide small boats to unload the ships. Lord Canning noted: "throughout the whole of the Naval arrangements great want of method" and concluded "that when there is anything more to be done by sea, the Naval Comr. in Ch. . . . shall stay at home."[27] Admiral Leeke sailed from Bushire for Bombay three days after the taking of Bushire, leaving Richard Ethersey, "Grim Dick", in command once more. "Heaven be praised," wrote Murray of Leeke's departure, "and Heaven grant that he may not honor the Gulf again by his presence."[28] He had quarrelled with everyone and his arrogance, vacillation and sheer incompetence had nearly ruined the attack on Bushire.

*

After the surrender of Bushire the British force settled down in camp outside the town walls, only two regiments being quartered in the town. A contemporary drawing of the scene looks idyllic. There are soldiers watering their horses, soldiers exercising, and a string of camels crossing the plain. A flock of white tents in the middle distance shelters the army, while offshore a haze of masts shows the fleet at anchor. Bushire appears to be a romantic walled city: and in the distance beyond the Bay of Bushire the mountains rise, capped with snow (see page 78). The weather was lovely, Lord Dunkellin wrote to his aunt, rather cold before sunrise, but warm as a fine English summer day during the daytime. The officers were eating very well: "news has just been brought of the arrival of a fine turtle for our mess . . . Lots of natives come about with milk, bread, oranges & vegetables. The fowls are large & very good, indeed it appears now that Bushire is famous for its fowls. The fish is good, & the *prawns* are nearly large enough to ride on."[29]

The townspeople of Bushire welcomed the sudden prosperity brought by the British force. The Armenians who had left the town at the declaration of war returned: they were the principal merchants and wealthiest inhabitants. Two Protestant churches were established in part of the Fort of Bushire, which was now renamed "Victoria City". A race-course was made, and one soldier mentions a railway built by the occupying force.[30] Lieutenant Brown and his regiment who were quartered in the town were busy cleaning it up, filling in numerous blind wells in the streets. It was a nasty dirty town, to his mind, and nearly every man he met had oppthalmia "and no wonder" he thought. They never washed or changed their clothes, but smoked themselves over a fire, which they said was a form of dry-cleaning – but even this only happened once a year. Surgeon Mills, who was in charge of the sappers' medical care, passed idle days in complaining about the soldiers' hypochondria, in going to church in the Anglican tent at least once a day and twice on Sundays, drinking tea with his friends and experimenting with photography with one of Eldred Pottinger's brothers.

Lord Dunkellin was under orders to report informally to

his uncle, Lord Canning, on the progress of the expedition. He was a good and amusing letter-writer, and when he had nothing of great importance to say to his uncle, he wrote to his aunt. On 16th December, 1856, for instance, he wrote: "I dedicate this despatch to you, as nothing of any material importance has occurred since I wrote to Uncle C. so I will not obtrude myself on his time. We are getting on very well tho' the excitement of fighting and new location being over, we are rapidly relapsing into the monotony of camp life. I have got a very good tent thanks to the General who is the best natured old man in the world, and having more than one of his own, has lent me a jolly Bengal Hill tent. It is much more convenient being on shore than living on board ship, as I am in the middle of everything and can see & hear what is going on much better than if I were afloat, besides at any rate here I am fixed, & feeling certain of my whereabouts, whereas I might be shifted from ship to ship according to the vacillating fancy of the Admiral in a most unpleasant manner. I hear that the General has sent in a flourishing account of our march on & capture of Bushire, & I am certain the Admiral has done the same. Many here, especially the young ones, are anxiously speculating on the chances of having a medal given for the business. If there be one granted from India pray do *you* choose the ribbon, and take care to let us have a pretty one that will look well on red & blue coats . . . I think a white ribbon with crimson edges wd. be tasty . . . I am rather disappointed in our spoil, especially in the horses. There are only four or five worth looking at; I shall try and get one at the Auction today . . . The loot in the way of dresses, cloths, carpets etc. etc. is not particular . . . I will try and get something to bring back for your room. The arms are dirty and worthless.

So I do not think there will be any large amount of prize money."[31]

Although superficially the expedition was well and happy, there were some underlying difficulties. The Commissariat provided little or no fodder for the horses, and the cavalry spent most of their time trying to keep their animals fed. Eventually the horses learned to eat, amongst other things, dates (dropping the stones out of their mouths) and cucumbers (5 lbs. a day, to cool their blood).[32] There was trouble too about water, the wells being brackish and used for the town as well as for the camp. Nearly all the townspeople of Bushire had to carry water home from wells two miles outside the town. This was a job usually done by the women of the family, who became very strong after years of this work. Several of the Baluchi soldiers married these girls who were nicknamed "Bushire packhorses".

Worst of all for the private soldiers was the continuing lack of local boats to carry goods from the ships to the shore. Every day half the troops had to report for fatigue duty to land provisions and camp equipment. The ships' boats were towed by the smaller steamers to within a couple of hundred yards of the beach; they were then towed farther in by dinghies and jolly boats; and when twenty or thirty yards from the shore the soldiers had to wade out to sea, up to their armpits in water, to unload them. Thereafter the loads had to be taken nearly two miles inland, through loose sand. One load a day was all that could be managed; and one load was a trifle in comparison with the needs of the force.

On New Year's Eve, 1856, General Stalker took the only other offensive measure of his command. He sent out a small party to destroy stores of flour and ammunition which he had learnt were at Chahkota, twenty miles away. The Sheikh of Chahkota, an Arab, was quite willing to give up the stores, but as there was a Persian Commissary in charge, he pretended to know nothing. "Whatever could have put such an idea into the head of General Stalker as to suppose that there was any magazine in the wretched little fort of Chahkota? The Colonel might look round and see," etc., etc. However when the Colonel threatened to burn the fort (which had the Sheikh's apartments in it), the magazine was quickly found, and the soldiers, helped by the villagers, carried the powder out into the plain so that the subsequent explosion did no harm to anyone, except perhaps the Persian Government. The villagers got most of the grain and flour, and the soldiers returned to camp for New Year's Day.[33]

General Stalker was worried about his force at Bushire. The mistakes of the Crimean War and the subsequent outcry against the generals haunted him. The temperature at night was now falling to 40°F. and the troops had no warm clothing. The days grew hotter and hotter, and unless the men were got into huts before long, to protect them from the extremes of temperature, they would become sick. The ceaseless fatigues in unloading the ships were wearing them out, and there were no spare men to fortify the exposed camp, lying wide open on a sandy plain with the sea at its back. Even though the Persians never attacked, there were always rumours of expected attacks to worry the general, and every day he could hear the morning gun of the undefeated force in the foothills. There was no chance at all that the present expedition would be able to move to the attack, off the coastal plain into the mountains or up the coast. Would the expedition become stuck with a port and a salient, like the Balaclava expedition? Stalker was trying to salvage his own private finances by gambling on the Bombay races.[34] To add to his troubles he was joined at Bushire by Charles Augustus Murray, recovering from a bad attack of boils and furious because he had not been given comprehensive powers to treat with the enemy.[35]

CHAPTER SIX

The Persian War – Khoosh-ab

SEVEN days after war was declared the Government of India learnt that the British Cabinet wished to extend operations in Persia and capture the town of Mohammerah* at the head of the Persian Gulf.[1] As this could not be carried out by the force already sailing for Persia unless greatly reinforced, the Indian Government began to gather further troops and a more experienced commander before the first ships were fairly under way. The war was gathering momentum. The troops already sailing to Persia were demoted from an army to merely a division, and as many troops again were warned for service, as a 2nd division. In the event the commander of both divisions applied for many more reinforcements as soon as he reached the Gulf, although at this time the expedition had hardly managed to find any Persians to fight: a nineteenth-century Parkinson's Law coming into operation ensuring that the army continued to grow in numbers. By the time this request reached the government, however, the war was over.

The new commander was Sir James Outram, who was to win a great reputation in the Indian Mutiny. In 1856 he had left India on sick leave, to all appearances a dying man. "He is quite broken down by illness. It is called acute rheumatism but it seems even worse . . . no one expects his return."[2] Lord Canning thought that twenty-four cigars a day might

* Now rebuilt as Khoramshahr.

be responsible for his illness. Now he was lying ill at Brighton. A soldier by training, Outram had spent much of his life on detached duty with the civil administration – a customary military practice which heavily depleted the staff of John Company's army. In 1856 he was Chief Commissioner of the newly annexed province of Oudh, but seeing a prospect of active service he brushed aside the immense difficulties of the Government of India in Oudh (which was soon to break into rebellion) and volunteered to command the army in Persia. He wrote to Lord Canning "in the supposition that I may be more usefully employed with the army about to proceed to Persia, than necessary to your lordship in Oude, where everything is progressing so satisfactorily, I have offered my services."[3] Lord Canning refused: "I do not therefore propose to avail myself of Genl. Outram's services in the Persian Gulf; and indeed I am glad not to be tempted to do so, for he is grievously wanted at Lucknow [capital of Oudh], where his locum tenens would by this time have exhausted my patience if it were not that the time of his relief is so near at hand – Mr. Jackson's facility in quarrelling with everybody, and in putting himself in the wrong, I have never seen equalled."[4] But in spite of Lord Canning's expressed wish, the Downing Street Cabinet decided to appoint Outram to Persia, with political as well as military powers. One of the East India Directors called on Outram at Brighton. "I am glad to see you," said the sick man, "for it may be the last time." "I am sorry for that," replied the Director, "for I had come to tell you that we had decided to offer you command of the expedition against Persia." "What! Persia?" exclaimed Outram, "I'll go tomorrow."[5] And go he did.

It is hard to know what to make of Outram. His unfinished portrait by Thomas Brigstocke[6] makes him look like a benign family doctor; wise, kind, with many anxieties which do not touch him too deeply. Lady Canning's description of him does not seem to fit his portrait at all "a very common looking little dark Jewish bearded man, with a desponding slow hesitating manner . . . he is not the least my idea of a hero."[7] His reputation as a soldier and as civil administrator was tremendous. He was called "The Bayard of India" and there was a Bombay saying, "A fox is a fool and a lion a coward by the side of Sir J. Outram."[8] His decision during the famous Relief of Lucknow to serve under his junior, General Havelock, who had already been fighting his way towards Lucknow for many weeks before Outram joined him, was a magnificent gesture. Yet having made it, he regretted it and thereafter constantly interfered with Havelock's command.[9] Many of his letters before, during and after the Mutiny show a conceit and a desire for self-glory which makes sickening reading. For instance, he persistently pressed the Government of India to grant him the Victoria Cross for his services in the Mutiny – over and over again he wrote, describing his prowess and claiming that the C.-in-C. was deliberately balking him of this honour.[10] He called his subsequent account of the Persian War *Lieut.-General Sir James Outram's Persian campaign*, and in the text as well as in the title managed to forget that Stalker originally commanded. He had many admirers, but also many enemies. To Lord Ellenborough he was "a Charlatan . . . no soldier . . . a correspondent of the Newspapers and owes his reputation to newspaper puffs."[11] Canning was suspicious of his efficiency as a peace-time administrator. "There is at bottom a radical inaptitude for the place in which he stands. How should it be otherwise with a man who has never been trained to Civil Administration. Unluckily, perhaps, for himself, but luckily for every one else, there has been no need of coercion, or of summary dealings with recalcitrant natives. If there had been, his peculiar merits and experience would, I do not doubt, have proved valuable."[12]

The commander of Outram's 2nd Division in Persia was Brigadier-General Henry Havelock, another man who was to win great fame in the Indian Mutiny. Outram is a contradiction, half "Charlatan" half hero; but Havelock is pure gold through and through: he conforms to the modern idea of a heroic soldier. Unlike Outram, who had spent much of his life in civilian posts, Havelock had always been a fighting soldier.

Henry Havelock was a very small man, 5 ft. 5 ins., who liked to point out that he was 5 ft. $5\frac{5}{16}$ ins.[13] He wanted to be a lawyer but the family money ran out and he was commissioned into the Rifle Brigade in the year of Waterloo. The money troubles which dogged him all his life soon led him to exchange his commission (no officer could live on his pay in the Rifle Brigade) for one in an Indian Regiment.

At this time promotion inside the Crown's regiments was almost entirely by purchase, each step having to be paid for by the aspiring officer. The rich prospered and became colonels, while the poor stayed lieutenants, saving their pay in the hope that they might one day buy a captaincy.[14] Indian Army commissions were not so socially desirable, and the death rate in India was high, even in peacetime. It was possible to gain promotion without purchase, though it took a very long time. Havelock was unlucky in his early career, and was forty-three before he became a captain, and gained the adjutancy of his regiment after he had been passed over by "3 sots and 2 fools".[15] After twenty-eight years of service he was still only a major and seemed likely to die in obscure poverty. But in the end his great experience of military life led to his appointment on the General Staff of the C.-in-C. India, and when the Persian War broke out he was a Lieutenant-Colonel and Adjutant-General.

The slowness of Havelock's rise in the army had been mostly due to poverty and bad luck – but partly due to his religious activities. He had been converted to the Baptist faith soon after his arrival in India, and had thereafter tried to live his life as a Christian soldier. This was a new concept in the Indian Army of his day, when drink, gambling, women and loot were the accepted recreations of the soldiers. As a lieutenant, Havelock held daily prayer meetings for all who wished to attend, and for this he was violently criticised. Later he founded an Army Temperance Movement.

In appearance Havelock was small, thin, with a handsome face and a fringe of beard. His poker back was often remarked on. Lady Canning wrote of him: "I knew him better almost than any one, and used to try and keep him in good humour when he seemed a little inclined to be affronted. He was very small, and upright, and stiff, very white and grey, and really like an iron ramrod. He always dined in his sword, and made his son do the same. He wore more medals than I ever saw on any one, and it was a joke that he looked as if he carried all his money round his neck. He certainly must have eleven or twelve of those great round half-crown pieces."[16]

Outram asked for Havelock as a Divisional Commander for Persia. They had met before, during the Afghan War, and admired each other very much. Havelock was delighted at the thought of active service and possible promotion, and accepted immediately, leaving Agra for his ship at such short notice and travelling so fast that his official transport never caught up with him. As he sailed out of Bombay harbour, the guns boomed out the salute due to his rank of Brigadier-General "the first expense of the kind to which I have ever put the Government."[17] He left all his medals in the bank at Agra and wrote to his wife to tell her so no less than three times.[18]

Havelock's division consisted of the 78th Highlanders (the Ross-shire Buffs, later the Seaforth Highlanders and eventually the Queen's Own Highlanders) the 23rd Bombay Native Infantry, the 26th Bombay Native Infantry, part of the 14th Light Dragoons* (now the 14/20th King's Hussars), some Horse Artillery, two field batteries and a light battalion of native troops from different regiments. An unexpected addition was a detachment of cavalry under Colonel John Jacob, the Commissioner of Sind. It was Jacob who refused help to Yar Mohammed Khan of Herat in 1856 and so embarrassed the government, then contemplating war. Since this débâcle, Jacob had made his peace with Lord Canning and had corresponded at length about the security of the North-West Frontier. It was Outram's idea that Jacob and the irregular cavalry, the Sind Horse, which he had raised and commanded, should go to Persia.

* The 14th Light Dragoons were at this time under a cloud. Led by William Havelock (brother of Henry) at Ramnagar (1848) in the 2nd Sikh war they lost a lot of men in a rash attack. At Chilianwala (1849), badly handled by the brigadier, they fled at the attack of some forty to fifty Sikh cavalry. It was suggested to Canning that he send the regiment

In the very first of his official letters, Outram asked for Jacob to be lent to him. Jacob believed the whole Persian campaign to be "enormous folly" and was loath to take even part of his Sind Horse from the Frontier. He was however persuaded to meet Outram, an old friend, at Bombay, and although he wrote sadly in his diary: "Heu! Quanto mutatus ab illo"[19] he agreed to go with Outram and to take 1,000 of his cavalry with him. He did not, however, leave Karachi until 6th March, long after Outram and most of the 2nd Division had reached Bushire.

One of the officers sent with the 2nd Division was Lieutenant George Digby Barker.[20] Like Henry Havelock he was a very small man, and only just scraped into the army at all – his uncle persuaded the C.-in-C. that his nephew, though under size, would probably grow some more once he was in the army. Whether he did so or not is not revealed, but in his portrait painted as a general he still looks very small.[21] Four months after joining the Army

to Persia with the 1st division to redeem itself. He replied that he did not propose to send the regiment to recover their good name as long as no regiment of the kind was wanted, and furthermore he did not want to send it under the command of Colonel Doherty. "At the time when the Expedition was put under orders, that Regiment was under the command of the officer who *ought* to have led it on at Chilianwala, and whom no one who had heard the story of that day, & knows the Estimation of that officer in India would dream of putting in the position of Commander of the whole Cavalry (wh. he would have been for the rest of the campaign) and next but one in rank to General Stalker himself. Colonel Doherty went to Europe in September; but he must have remained if his Regiment had been selected for service. Possibly he may now return (as the 14th are under orders) and the chance of this is a strong reason amongst others for making Colonel Jacob a Brigadier General." (Canning Papers: Letters to the President of the Board of Control, 48, 8th January, 1857.)

Bushire

The expedition's camp and the town of Bushire

General Sir James Outram

General Sir Henry Havelock

The camp of Borasjoon

The battle of Khoosh-ab

he was sent to Poona, where the 78th Highlanders were stationed. He was a hard-working boy, and in a letter to his mother gives his time-table for a working day – only two hours of his time were spent on military duties (two drill periods), but he spent many hours learning native languages voluntarily, as much as nine hours a day, six days a week, on Marathi.[22]

By New Year's Day, 1857, there were many reports that the 78th were to leave for Persia – on the strength of these rumours, Barker ordered a revolver from England. But it reached him far too late for the Persian War, for on 6th January, at sunset, the regiment was suddenly ordered to march for Bombay at 3 a.m. the next morning. Barker managed to stay an extra day at Poona, during which time he had to "sell all my furniture, pay all bills, wish good-bye to all friends, perambulate Poona to find some public-spirited individual to succeed me as Honorary Secretary and Treasurer to the Poona Gymkhana Club, and having caught him hand over all the accounts, stores, kit, and funds belonging to it, to have our Officers' Library, of which I am Secretary, packed up and placed in Store, to pack up my marching kit, and what is called by good ladies in England to 'go shopping' for various articles necessary for a campaign."[23]

On 19th January, the 78th Highlanders left the harbour of Bombay, with the band playing and the colours flying. Barker was in the steamship *Precursor* towing two sailing ships carrying the 26th Native Infantry, and the left wing of the 78th was in the *Pottinger* towing two more sailing ships containing the 78th recruits, heavy baggage and horses. Such was the shortage of steamers that they had to be made use of in this curious way: *Precursor* and *Pottinger* towed their transports all the way to Bushire, a journey which took eleven days.[24]

There also sailed in the *Precursor*, Corporal John Borthwick of the 78th, whose worries were quite different from Barker's. He worried mostly about his wife and sons, left behind at Poona with ten rupees a month to spend – about £1. Like any soldier in any age no one had told him where he was going, or when, or why, or for how long. In the ship in Bombay harbour he wrote to his wife that his friend Sergeant Crosbie and his wife Margaret wanted Mrs Borthwick and the children to spend a few months with them at Bombay: "it is very kind of them but I think you are better where you are as you know that you have no person to take care of the Children going on the road . . . Margaret is pretty fickle minded. So they might get tired of you and it would be only expenses."[25]

Outram himself, the new commander of the whole force, travelled separately, there being some difficulty about his rank. In the mid-nineteenth-century army, seniority was of enormous importance, and Stalker, in command at Bushire, was senior to Outram in the Army List by a very short head – they had in fact joined the army on the same day, thirty-seven years before. To enable Outram to command he was given a special *local* rank of Lieutenant-General, to apply to Persia only. But the first notification of this from the Horse Guards granted the rank "in the East Indies", and as Stalker might have refused to accept that this applied to Persia, Outram had to wait until a more accurate commission came through.

Outram overtook the slow progress of *Precursor* and *Pottinger* with their trains of sailing ships and landed at Bushire on 27th Janury, 1857, to find himself in a potentially dangerous situation. The army was still encamped on its beachhead, still humping supplies up the shore. The entrenchment round the camp was a simple ditch about three feet deep and six feet wide, with a parapet of the earth dug out of the ditch, and batteries at the angles and salient points. A cavalry picket, about two miles to the front, was the only outpost.[26] Against this peaceful settlement the Persians were planning a great attack to drive the infidel into the sea. The C.-in-C. of the Persian army, Sooja-ool-Moolk, had formed an entrenched camp at Borasjoon, about forty-six miles inland from Bushire, under the mountains. Here he had about 7,000 troops and eighteen guns, with promised reinforcements of twelve regiments, and thirty-five guns.[27]

Outram was never a man to waste time. He did not copy the leisurely disembarkation of the 1st Division, but somehow got his troops off the ships and marching against Borasjoon in three days: Havelock had not yet arrived. Of course it was very risky. The force he took was just over 4,500 men and eighteen guns, with supplies for three days. Bushire was guarded in his absence by less than 2,000 men.[28]

The remaining garrison watched their comrades march out of the camp in two columns. They were a colourful sight, most of the troops being Bombay native infantrymen. Each regiment had a distinctive uniform, vying with each other in their peacock colours, no concession being made to camouflage or comfort. For instance, the 2nd Bombay Europeans wore red with facings of white, the lace white and caps with a green silk ball like a tuft, and the 78th Highlanders wore (whatever the temperature) red woollen jackets with Mackenzie kilts or tartan trews and glengarries.

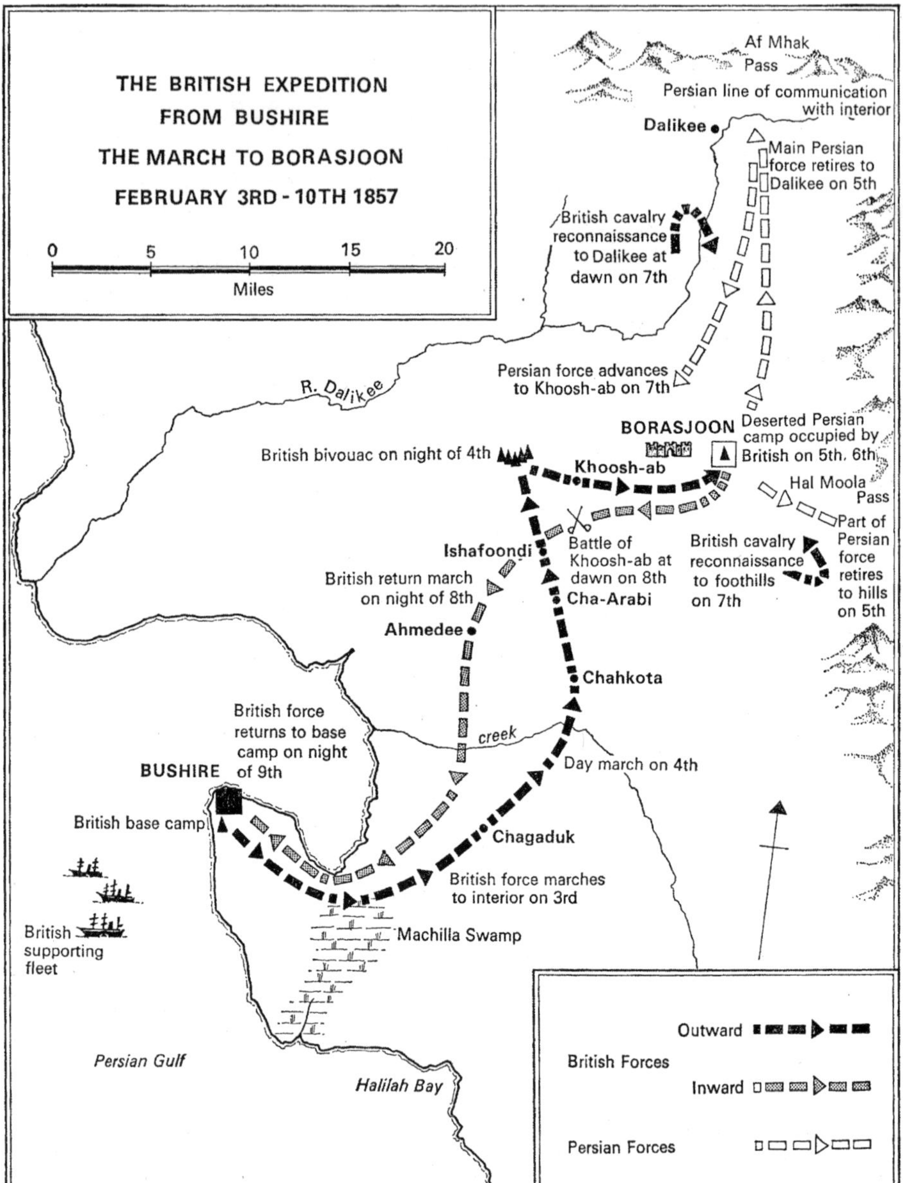
THE BRITISH EXPEDITION
FROM BUSHIRE
THE MARCH TO BORASJOON
FEBRUARY 3RD - 10TH 1857
0 5 10 15 20
Miles
Af Mhak Pass
Persian line of communication with interior
Dalikee
Main Persian force retires to Dalikee on 5th
British cavalry reconnaissance to Dalikee at dawn on 7th
R. Dalikee
Persian force advances to Khoosh-ab on 7th
BORASJOON
Deserted Persian camp occupied by British on 5th, 6th
British bivouac on night of 4th
Khoosh-ab
Hal Moola Pass
Part of Persian force retires to hills on 5th
Battle of Khoosh-ab at dawn on 8th
British cavalry reconnaissance to foothills on 7th
Ishafoondi
British return march on night of 8th
Cha-Arabi
Ahmedee
Chahkota
British force returns to base camp on night of 9th
creek
BUSHIRE
Day march on 4th
British base camp
Chagaduk
British force marches to interior on 3rd
British supporting fleet
Machilla Swamp
Persian Gulf
Halilah Bay
British Forces
Outward
Inward
Persian Forces

The soldiers had no tents or cover of any kind, just their greatcoats and a blanket apiece, and the journey was hellish. They carried two days' cooked rations and the Commissariat had a further two or three days' provisions. Surgeon Mills took with him a supply of cold roast fowls, bread, tea, sugar and a bottle of brandy, his Scotch rug, plaid and a blanket, a large amount of warm underclothes, his sword and his revolver. Because Sir James Outram's campaigning had always been in India, he always made the army march at night: nobody liked it and it was thought by officers and men to be quite unnecessary, as it was now winter in Persia and quite tolerable in the daytime. But they marched at night, in pitch darkness so that a man would hardly know where the column was, through sand and swamps. The first day's rest was spent trying vainly to find cover from a dust storm. The army marched again at four in the afternoon, through deep sand most tiring to march in. "Men at last began to fall by dozens, worn out from fatigue, till the General found it necessary to halt for fear of having no army with him. We halted about 10.30 p.m. and threw ourselves down on a sandbank to sleep, but we hardly laid down when a violent thunderstorm came on, rain poured in floods and soaked us to the skins; thus we lay all night."[29] Surgeon Mills and the Anglican padre tried to build a shelter out of sand, a carpet and blankets, but the violence of the storm washed down the sand walls, and they had a miserable night and no breakfast.

On the morning of 5th February, the exhausted army at last saw the Persian Army in front of Borasjoon. Now the cumbersome drill began to manœuvre into battle order, a short halt took place to get the regiments into their different positions for attack, when to the disgust of all the whole

Persian army was seen to be retreating. The British force occupied the Persian camp and took a lot of spoil.

Two days were spent at Borasjoon, a slightly fortified camp outside a village, under the formidable ramparts of the mountains which guarded the upland plateau of Persia. A picture by Captain Hunt (78th Highlanders) shows a little group of Highlanders, in tartan trews, apparently enjoying a quiet smoke and a cup of tea behind a windbreak. Many other soldiers are standing about, apparently aimlessly. There is at least one tent visible, perhaps that of Outram himself? (see page 79).

No attacks were made by the Persians at Borasjoon, though one night some reconnoitring was done, and all the troops were made to stand to arms. It was a nerve-racking business waiting in the dark in an unknown place for an unseen enemy – the picket of one regiment captured a door which was leaning against a bush in a suspicious manner, and a battle nearly broke out between two groups each taking the other for the enemy.

On Friday, 6th February, Outram ordered the army to try to catch the Persians at the mouth of the passes which loomed over Borasjoon – "the order was fortunately rescinded – I believe Sir James Outram was dissuaded from carrying it out by the whole of his staff, who, as the events proved, were wiser than he, had we gone I believe not a man would have returned to tell the tale. The Persians were all ready for us, and wished only to entice us to their hills where they would have massacred the whole of us."[30]

On the evening of the 7th, the troops, by now short of rations and tired out by uncomfortable nights and the fear of alarums, began to retrace their steps to Bushire, having achieved nothing but a show of force. An officer was left behind to fire the huge quantity of explosive which had been captured from the Persians. This he did with one of Jacob's new patent rifles, but "unfortunately, he did not wait until the force was far enough away – the bullets and bits of shell fell about like hailstones, wounding several officers and men, and driving the horses wild with fright. The night was very dark – well suited for such a display of fireworks – and the rush of the mighty column of flame into heaven, with clouds of white silvery smoke, mingled with shells bursting like rockets, attended by a report that made the hills echo again and again, and a concussion that shook the earth for miles, formed a beautiful sight, which I shall never forget."[31]

As the British retired towards Bushire, the Persians were thought to have retreated over the mountains, and there was no fear of an attack. Suddenly just after midnight the rear-guard of the army was attacked, and after about half an hour the whole force was surrounded by yelling, shooting Persians – it must have been rather like the traditional Red Indian attack on the waggon train. An added confusion for the British was that the Persians, having been trained by European officers, knew the bugle calls, and in front of the 78th Highlanders the Persians sounded "Cease Fire" and then "Incline to the Left".[32] The 20th Native Infantry on the other hand thought that it was their own force firing on them so they sounded the "Cease Fire" and the Persians fired a salvo and then stopped firing in that direction.

When the first shots were fired at the rear of the column, Outram had immediately set off at a gallop to find out what the trouble was. But in the dark his horse stumbled and threw him, and he was unconscious for several hours. Command devolved on General Stalker and Outram's Chief of Staff, Colonel Lugard, who had the task of trying to deal with an unseen enemy. The British troops were at first "much distracted and alarmed" and some guns opened fire at random. This was so dangerous in the dark that Lugard (a very sensible and cool officer, who played a great part in calming down Outram's wilder schemes) ordered all firing to stop. The Persians however continued to fire, and at about 4 a.m. the 3rd Bombay Light Cavalry was ordered by an Engineer Officer to "go and take those guns": unlike the order which led to the charge of the Light Brigade three years before, it was tacitly ignored.[33] *Two-thirds* of the British troops had never been under fire before, but for the rest of the hours of darkness they held steady. In the face of the enemy's fire they were rearranged from their marching order (columns) to form an oblong, a brigade on each flank, a demi-brigade to the front and rear, guns at intervals, and a thick line of skirmishers covering all, with the baggage and the numerous camp followers in the centre. When the oblong was completed, the troops lay down in their places and waited for the dawn, enduring the ordeal of the slow bouncing roundshot as best they might. Surgeon Mills spent most of the night watching the unconscious Outram, wondering whether he should bleed him or not.

Dawn came at last, and as a sharp cold wind cleared away the mist, the Persian army was seen, drawn up for battle. There were over 6,000 Persian soldiers stretching in a long thin line, their right resting on the walled village of Khoosh-ab and their left on a hamlet with a small fortified tower. On either flank there were groups of cavalry, very picturesque in flowing green and red robes. The commander was the C.-in-C. of the Persian Army, Sooja-ool-Moolk, aided by the Eel-Khanee, the chief of the nomad tribes of the region.

THE BATTLE OF KHOOSH-AB

THE POSITION AT DAWN 8TH FEBRUARY, 1857

0 — 1 Miles

26	26th Bombay Native Infantry	3HA	3rd Horse Artillery
78	78th Highlanders	3	3rd Light Battery
2B	2nd Baluchi Battalion	5	5th Light Battery
20	20th Bombay Native Infantry	4R	4th Rifles
64	64th Regt.	2E	2nd European Light Infantry
PH	Poona Horse	3B	3rd Bombay Light Cavalry

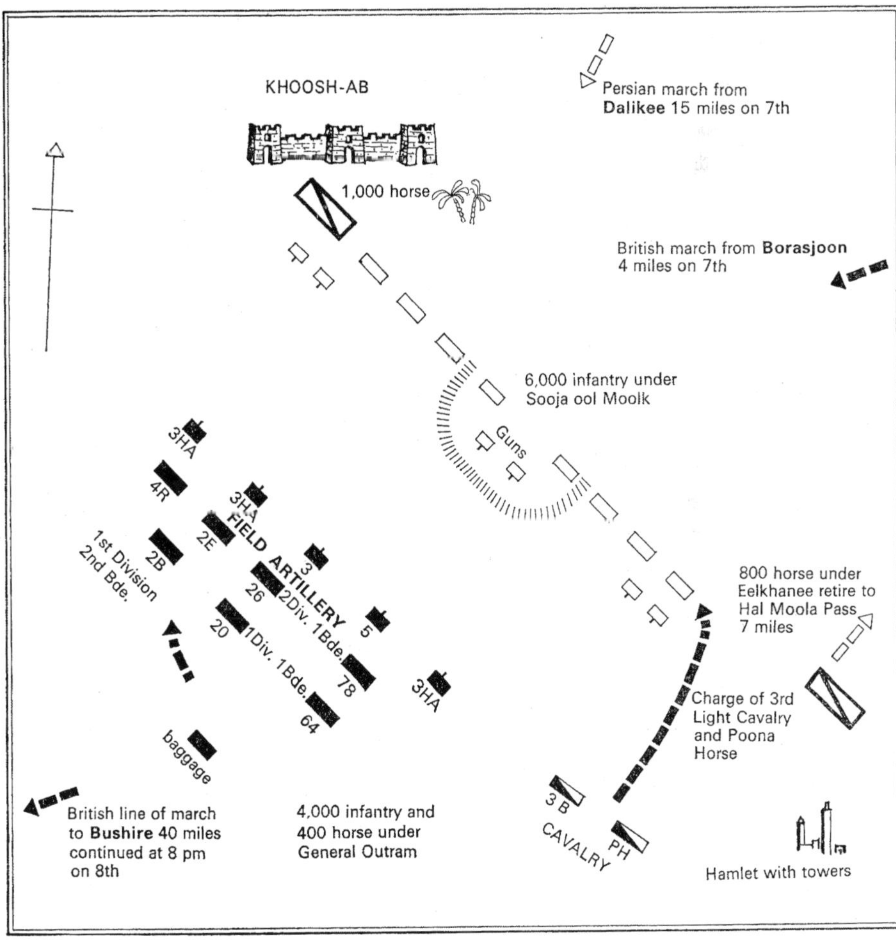

Captain Hunt has left an impression of the opening of the battle of Khoosh-ab. In the background the mountains rise out of the plain in huge steps. The ground is sandy desert with scattered palm trees and here and there a few little windowless houses. Puffs of smoke mark some actual fighting, in the middle ground of the picture. In the foreground there is a most remarkable scene: great numbers of British troops are not in the battle at all, but are marching about in a parade ground style, some of them actually marching away from the enemy (see page 79). The force had kept its oblong formation all night long. Now that day had come, it was necessary to rearrange the troops into their battle order – and this took a long time. In Hunt's words: "The outward formation of our infantry brigades, to protect the baggage and followers over-night, rendered some manœuvring and a change of front to the original direction of march necessary, as the enemy's line interposed to the north-east. This was soon affected, the regiments countermarching, and deploying on their rear divisions. This, in some measure, transposed the position of brigades, as the first brigade of the first division, which had been, during the night, in advance of the first brigade, second division, was now placed in rear of it; but all the regiments moving up as they successively deployed, two general lines were formed."[34] All this was done at a stately march, while the cavalry and the artillery were engaging the enemy.

The cavalry had begun their action at first light. The Poona Irregular Horse saw, in the dawn, a large body of infantry forming up into line on their right: there was no time to wait for orders, so the commander immediately ordered the attack and the Poona Horse broke and scattered the enemy's 1st Kushkai Regiment of Fars.[35]

Cornet Combe was waiting with the 3rd Bombay Light Cavalry to the left of the Poona Horse. It had been a long cold night, and at dawn he was longing to be moving. "We had not long to wait. Forbes, giving the order to mount, put himself at our head, and gave the order: 'The line will advance. Draw swords. Third squadron. Walk. Trot. Gallop' and when within a hundred yards of the enemy 'Charge!' " The 3rd Bombay Cavalry crashed into a square of Persian infantry, the unbreakable square that they had learnt from the British, the front two ranks kneeling and their comrades firing over their heads, the square that had won Waterloo. Colonel Forbes and his Adjutant Moore led the way. Moore's horse swerved – he dropped his sword, let it hang by its knot at his wrist, and with both hands screwed his horse's head straight and as if taking a fence out hunting jumped him straight on to the square. The horse fell dead upon the bayonets. Behind Moore rode his elder brother, eighteen stone and six foot seven inches high, and his two companions Lieutenant Malcolmson and Lieutenant Spens, riding shoulder to shoulder and spurring on their horses as if pig-sticking. As the younger Moore and his dead horse crashed to the ground his sword broke, and his life was saved by Malcolmson, who fought his way to his side through a solid mass of Persians, gave him a stirrup to hang on to and carried him clear away from the square. The formation of the square now broke up, and the Indian troopers crashed right through, re-formed on the other side, and crashed back again, shouting "Ali, Ali." Colonel Forbes was shot in the hip, two men were killed and ten wounded. Cornet Combe's horse was wounded in five places (but recovered, and was subsequently called Khoosh-ab) and he himself had a very narrow escape, three musket balls lodging in a "guernsey" that he carried over his pistol holster. The Persians were thought to have lost nearly the whole square, 500 men . . .[36] Thus was destroyed the 1st Regular Regiment of Fars. This feat, the breaking of a square of infantry, was a great delight to the military experts as it had formerly been considered impossible for cavalry to break such a square of steady infantry.[37] For their part in this action the younger Moore (A. T. Moore, Lieutenant and Adjutant, 3rd Bombay Light Cavalry) and J. G. Malcolmson (Lieutenant, 3rd Bombay Light Cavalry), were awarded the Victoria Cross.[38]

The battle was over before the double line of infantry, finishing their marching and counter-marching, had time to fight. They marched steadily towards the Persian line, but at the last minute the Persians broke and almost the entire force fled, throwing away as they ran, their arms and even their clothes. The officers, being mounted, fled first and farthest.

The Persians lost 700 men on the battlefield and a great many more were killed as they tried to escape across the plain. The troopers and irregular cavalry "were fairly exhausted cutting down the fugitives."[39] This massacre was considered permissible because the Persians often tried to kill their captors, even after they had been granted quarter, and they always killed any of the invading force they found. Many muskets were captured, two brass nine-pounders and a standard with a silver hand on the pike staff. The British force lost only nineteen killed and sixty-four wounded.

The battle of Khoosh-ab was fought on a Sunday (as was the battle of Waterloo, though there was not otherwise much resemblance between the two battles). By 10 a.m. it was all over. The surviving Persians, their C.-in-C. and their guns, had withdrawn into the mountains. The British could only return to Bushire, short of food, short of sleep and now tireder than ever. About noon it began to rain, and it rained all the way back to Bushire. In accordance with Outram's theories the troops did not march off the battlefield until evening, and bivouacking on the ground where they had fought was anything but pleasant, with the Persian dead lying about, many of them burning, having been set on fire by the muskets and cartridges.

About eight o'clock in the evening the column moved off the field and marched all night. In spite of the rain there was not enough water to drink until the force reached Chagaduk, twenty-two miles from Borasjoon; the roads were almost impassable with sticky mud, the shoes of the infantry were sucked off their feet by the mud and many soldiers came back bare-foot. They became so exhausted that they threw away their kit, and the wayside was littered with the debris of the army, clothes and weapons. The mud was half clay and sand, and over ankle deep; yet, through this, and drenched to the skin, the column marched through the hours of darkness. The guide, either from treachery or ignorance, misled the force, and about four in the morning a halt took place in consequence, to wait for daylight. There in the midst of pitiless rain, sunk knee-deep, and in a biting northerly wind, two long weary hours were passed, without even a tree in sight, and the swamp around looking in the hazy light like a vast lake. Men and officers alike stretched themselves in the mire, and tried to rest.[40]

At Chagaduk there was food for the troops, sent out from Bushire, and water; but by now the men were so miserable that the C.O.s of the regiments asked to be allowed to go on. Outram agreed and took the incredible risk of splitting his force and left it optional to each Commanding Officer to move on when his men were sufficiently rested – "all precautions against an enemy being superfluous, with the certain information I possessed of the flight of the Persians in a contrary direction. The late hour, however, at which some of the Regiments recommenced their march led to an occurrence upon which camp alarmists, and those ignorant of the state of affairs, have apparently grounded their false reports; some of the camp followers strayed from the line of march and in the dark losing their way upon the marsh discharged the Persian muskets they had picked up on the field of battle, as signals of distress!"[41] The men came back to camp in a dreadful state, covered with mud and reeling with exhaustion, dropping to the ground as they entered camp. The first-comers believed that the enemy were attacking the rear of the army, and as the camp followers kept letting off their muskets, the artillery were kept at their guns till nearly midnight. At midnight the gunners went to pick up those still straggling round the camp – men too exhausted to move, or those wounded who had been abandoned by their nervous stretcher-bearers. One of those that fell out of the army was Corporal John Borthwick, "my thighs failed me . . . some thousands fell out of our Army it was an awful march the like was never known in the Annals of British history."[42] Next morning the rear-guard came into the Bushire camp, the cavalry very pleased with themselves, calling "Dekho Sahib" and showing off their swords caked with blood and their white belts all splashed with red.

Outram's enemies saw this retreat from Khoosh-ab as a panic-stricken retreat, followed closely by the enemy. Outram was sure that it was a glorious victory – but after the battle fewer supplies of food came in for the British, the local merchants were no longer so sure that the British would win.

The Persian Army was disheartened by this battle, and a spy for Outram reported that the Persian C.-in-C. had fled to Khisht without his troops, and had been superseded. The Persian soldiers complained that the officers had run away and deserted them during the battle, but not only the officers had run away. A Persian cavalry commander who had been at Khoosh-ab told the story, many years later, of how during the battle he and his 800 men had managed to isolate one trooper of a lancer regiment. But, he said, "That madman of a lancer was not in the least frightened: he couched his lance and charged the whole of us, and, of course, we all ran away, firing as we fled."[43]

There were so many Persians dead after Khoosh-ab that they had to be buried in pits, and after the battle the C.-in-C. wrote despondently to the Shah that his army was broken up, and unless the Shah sent men to hold the passes all was lost. But another chief sent the Shah a glowing report of Persian successes and British losses, and the C.-in-C. cheered by the British retreat changed his tone and declared that it was quite true that he had fought like Rustem. The Shah sent him a dress of honour, but nevertheless decided he should be replaced. The Sadr Azim, sitting like a spider in Teheran, knew very well that there was going to be no military glory for Persia in the war, and that the new C.-in-C. would be blamed for the inevitable defeat. So he replaced the C.-in-C. elect, who happened to be his nephew, by a particular enemy of his, the commander of the royal bodyguard, whose splendid title was Sirkesheck-chee Bashi, in the hope that he would be disgraced. The

Sirkesheckchee Bashi (who was nicknamed "Cheeky Bashi" by the British troops) set off for war with the equipment of 50,000 tomans (about £22,500), fifty gold-mounted swords, a case full of decorations and several loads of shawls and robes of honour. But he took care to travel so slowly that the war was lost before ever he reached the Persian Army.[44]

For days after the battle of Khoosh-ab it rained, and at Bushire the British Force slept exhausted amidst mud in their sodden tents. In fair intervals they played cricket and organised races. Food for the men and fodder for the horses grew shorter. Every day each regiment had to lend 300 men to the engineers who were building five redoubts to guard the camp. Rumours ran through the lines that the General was going to attack again "Mormong or some Name like that Some strong Fort about 48 hours sailing"[45] Outram had indeed already decided to attack again, this time at the head of the Gulf – Mohammerah.

CHAPTER SEVEN

The Persian War – Mohammerah

THE capture of Bushire and the battle of Khoosh-ab had not brought about the desired result, it had not forced the Shah to surrender, he had not withdrawn from Herat nor withdrawn his comments on Charles Augustus Murray. He had in fact sent an ambassador to treat for peace, to Constantinople and later to Europe, but this was considered insufficient reason to halt the progress of the campaign. The invading force therefore moved to attack their next objective, the town of Mohammerah, at the north end of the Persian Gulf, at the junction of two great rivers. By taking this town Outram hoped to ensure supplies from the west and especially baggage animals, which could not be got in sufficient quantities while the Persians held Mohammerah.

Outram was held at Bushire by the non-arrival of reinforcements from India (the rest of the 2nd Division). The wind was blowing steadily from the north-west, from nine in the morning until sundown, and the same wind which was forcing the troop transports to tack up the Gulf brought misery to the encamped soldiers. A fine sand blew everywhere, even through the tent walls, covering everything, making washing and dressing a burden and a walk against the wind a cruel punishment.[1] Outram filled in the waiting time with extra inspections of the regiments, and the completion of strong defences around the camp. General Havelock, who had just arrived, wrote to his wife of the

10-foot square tent he shared with his son, and of their two iron camp beds. Life was boring – "our encampment on a sandy plain surrounded with entrenchments, in front of a small Asiatic town with its grey stone curtains & round towers, and a horizon of sea & date trees is not very lively . . ."[2] Meanwhile Corporal Borthwick of the 78th Highlanders was complaining more forcibly to his wife (he shared a tent with twenty-nine soldiers) about the sand, the cold, the wind and the disgusting food "rations of the worse description Mutton they call it but I think it is Dead Parah Dogs our meat is Bad Cooked generally More sand and flies than Mutton and Soup. No Vegatables for Soup but Onions and 3 small potatoes each man with about 1 onion for each man cut up among the soup they call it, and bad water, very salt . . . the sooner this war is settled the better but we don't know when for everything is kept very dark, only Outram is the only one that knows untill it is done."[3]

Four weeks after the battle of Khoosh-ab the north-wester at last slackened, and the swell and surf off Bushire died down. Outram decided not to wait for the transports, and began to embark his troops, about 4,000 men, for the head of the Gulf. He planned to leave General Stalker in command of a garrison of about 3,000 men at Bushire.

On 6th March, the first ships put to sea and the same day three steamers arrived from India with some Horse Artillery and part of the Sind Horse. The same steamers brought General Stalker the results of the Bombay races.[4] A spy report was also brought in from the plateau above Bushire, that the Persian Army, now considerably reinforced, was about to advance, presumably on the lightly defended Bushire. Once more the enemy's camp fires were seen on the hills around the camp at night.[5]

John Jacob, now a temporary Brigadier-General, arrived at Bushire on 13th March with the remainder of the Sind Horse. He was very shocked by the confusion he found in the camp, and blamed it all on Outram: he wrote in his diary: "Sir James Outram appears to me to be in his second childhood. I can imagine no greater political crime than that which has been committed by those who have entrusted an English Army and the most important interests of our country to a General in such a state of health. Nothing appears to remain in Sir James Outram's mind but a morbid sense of the opinions of others, his brain appears to have degenerated into one immense organ of love of approbation and I find no response to any great or good idea when I endeavour to rouse him to better thoughts; while orders and counter orders are every hour issued by the General, all departments are confused and everyone is disgusted."[6] The Chief of Staff he praised: "I find Col. Lugard one of the most excellent men and best soldiers I have ever met with – able, energetic, cool and methodical – it is evident to me that his presence alone has saved this army from some great disaster. But I can well imagine what he must have suffered from the miserable proceedings of the General prior to my arrival here."[7]

That same evening that Jacob arrived Outram and Stalker took their walk together, as was their custom. Stalker had apparently reconciled himself to his supersession, and he had insisted that Outram be his guest and share his tent.[8] But as he walked through the camp his mind was full of troubles. His health had suffered during the nightmare return from Khoosh-ab. His personal finances were in chaos and his attempt to salvage them by gambling on the Bombay races had failed. Sick, poor, superseded, he was now to be left in charge of Bushire with what even Outram called an insufficient force.[9] Stalker tried to get more cavalry at least, but Outram refused to allow him any.

In the morning Stalker asked his A.D.C. to load his pistols and said he must put them in a safe place "or else someone will be shooting himself." After breakfast he went into his tent and blew his brains out.[10]

*

On 15th March, after a hasty inquest, Stalker was declared to have died by his own hand in a fit of temporary insanity and was buried with full military honours, minute guns and the Dead March, "a most injudicious proceeding in my opinion" wrote Jacob.[11] The command had to be reorganised rapidly, because half the force for Mohammerah had already sailed. Jacob was to be left in charge at Bushire, whilst Outram and Havelock went with the force to the head of the Gulf. On 17th March, Jacob went to see Sir James who was due to leave that day for Mohammerah. Since Stalker's death he had not lived in the camp but in the Residency at Bushire, where Jacob found him still in bed. Before Outram had time to dress news was brought in that the Commander of the Gulf Squadron, Commodore Ethersey, had shot himself during the night. Sir James "went into a fit and behaved like a child".[12] Ethersey's body was found beside an official reprimand from the C.-in-C. of the Indian Navy, his old enemy Sir Henry Leeke. He was completely worn out by his responsibilities and believed he was unfit for command; the entries in his diary showed that Stalker's suicide had suggested a way out. Poor Grim Dick. Jacob was as usual disgusted with his chief's behaviour and wrote in his diary: "Sir James Outram cross-questioned

Jones [Felix Jones, the Resident] in our presence with a view to prove that he (Sir James) had not driven Ethersey to commit suicide by vexatious interference, etc. This was a painful exhibition and tended to produce exactly the contrary effect to that which was intended by it."[13]

The two suicides cast a gloom over the whole expedition. Both men, Stalker and Ethersey, were excessively worried by the responsibilities devolving on them in what had been a successful expedition. The shadow of the Crimea hung over them. For the terrible conditions at Balaclava and before Sebastopol scapegoats were still being found, and the generals of the Crimean War, even the C.-in-C., Lord Raglan, had been hounded by the Press. In Persia the troops were in danger of their lives, not so much from the Persians as from the climate and their lack of equipment. Stalker had worried about getting the European troops out of tents into huts before the hot weather began to kill them. Ethersey worried about the naval transport service, which had also been greatly criticised after the Crimean War. "They did not quail in action. It was in the quiet tent, pondering over 'what they would say in England' that they broke down."[14]

The first part of the force for Mohammerah had by now been at the head of the Gulf for nearly two weeks and Outram still could not leave to join them. A number of the expedition's ships were anchored in the mouth of the Euphrates, and here on board the soldiers remained. The Persians would come down to the water's edge, and both sides looked at each other with curiosity – yet no shots were fired unless the ships' boats went too near the shore.

All along the northern shores of the Gulf the staple food was dates. Men lived on dates, and so did horses, dogs and camels. Even the little foxes ate dates, not jumping up to take them off the palms, but waiting until the wind blew the ripe fruit down.[15] The part of the Euphrates in which the ships lay was flat and dull. From the sea the river mouth was marked by huge flocks of pelicans and very tall bulrushes; the shores were studded with primitive mud villages, planted in swamp and backed by date palms. The river was very muddy, and, an observer thought, about as wide as the Thames at Tilbury Fort. Every year when the mountain snows melted the river flooded for a few weeks, and when the flood waters receded, crops were grown in the mud. To the marsh Arabs the floods and the mud were the corner-stone of their existence, but to foreigners the season after the flood was very dangerous – the rich mud brought malaria and fever.

Life on board the ships was very monotonous. The soldiers could not land on the west bank of the river, because it was Turkish and the British Government was anxious to preserve Turkish neutrality. They could not land on the east bank without clashing with the Persians. So overcrowded, short of food, they waited and waited, while the Persians practised manœuvres on shore and worked frantically to strengthen their defences upstream.

The small muddy town of Mohammerah lay on the Karun river just above its junction with the Shatt-al-Arab, the confluence of the Tigris and the Euphrates.[16] The Karun here ran east-west, and at the junction of the rivers the Persians had erected two large batteries, one on each bank of the Karun. The walls of the batteries were made of earth only but were enormously thick, about eighteen feet thick and tapering upwards to a height of about eighteen to twenty-five feet. The gun embrasures were strengthened with the trunks of date trees, a very solid wood which did not splinter, and the interiors of the forts were studded with pits full of water to catch the enemy's shot.[17] As well as the two main forts there were a number of smaller batteries and entrenchments. The town lay behind the fortifications, and was further protected by an army of about 13,000 under the command of Prince Khanler Mirza. The guns of the forts commanded all the approaches by water, and the land between and behind the forts was full of groves of date-palms and mud creeks which filled at high tide.

The British had looked at the fortifications several times before the war started and were well aware of their strength. Captain Maisonneuve with the French frigate *Sybille* was in the Gulf (his ship was draped in mourning because the remains of his father-in-law were on board). He had visited the Persian camp at Mohammerah a short time before and had inspected all the fortifications: rather unfairly, it seems, he hastened to describe them to the British. He told Outram that he thought they were very formidable and that if he attacked Outram would lose three steamers at least.[18] Since the British ships had been lying in the Euphrates, the Persians had been working day and night to strengthen the forts.

Meanwhile at Bushire, Outram had left Jacob in charge with only one little brig, the *Euphrates*, to assist him. The *Euphrates* had originally joined the expedition as a surveying ship and was commanded by Lieutenant C. G. Constable, son of John Constable, R.A., the landscape painter. He was an excellent surveyor and friend of Sir John Outram, for whom he had drawn maps in Egypt. His knowledge of every creek and inlet of the Gulf was so profound that it had become proverbial amongst his brother officers.[19] Now he took his ship up Bushire creek, crossed top-gallant yards to make a brave show, borrowed three thirty-two-pounders from the *Clive* and prepared to deal with the Persian attack, daily expected.[20] At the same time he made a careful survey of Bushire creek and Bushire harbour.

The troops left with Jacob were twelve companies of infantry, drawn from four regiments, some artillery, and all the 1st Division cavalry – in fact all that the unfortunate Stalker had wanted. Outram could not decide what to do with the Sind Horse – he sent a detachment to Mohammerah, then recalled them, then sent them back to Mohammerah again, but forgot to send their baggage.[21]

At last, on 21st March, 1857, General Outram and the headquarter staff joined the attacking force in the river Euphrates. He had yet one more obstacle to deal with: Mohammerah was a somewhat awkward place to attack politically, as the Turks had once owned it, and just before Outram came up the river the Turks protested against any attack because the town was disputed territory.[22] A small Turkish brig-of-war was anchored in the river leading to Mohammerah. A few days before attacking, therefore, Outram sent a political officer to ask the Turks to be good enough to remove their ship for the time being, so that the attacking force could pass. The Turkish claims to Mohammerah were to be answered: "should the British, however, capture the place, their tenure of it will not interfere with any just claims upon it which the Government of Her Majesty may recognize on the part of his Imperial Majesty the Sultan."[23] This manœuvre was effective.

On 23rd March, the whole force moved upriver to the attack. The more fantastic of Outram's plans such as "the infantry should advance, and taking the Southern battery in reverse storm it by its gorge" and "14 field artillery guns only should be horsed, and the remainder moved by hand" were modified on the advice of Havelock[24] and the scheme eventually agreed upon was that the navy would shell the forts until their fire was silenced, or almost so, when the troops would be landed above the northern battery so as to attack the Persian camp and the town of Mohammerah.

*

As darkness fell on the eve of battle, a small raft made o casks and studding-sail booms lashed together was quietly towed to within a few hundred yards of the northern battery. Here all night a small band of British artillerymen waited in silence, a "forlorn hope" protected from the powerful guns of the fort only by their silence and a boat full of hay anchored in front of them. The raft carried four mortars.

The soldiers' thoughts that night were of their homes and their mortality. Lieutenant Barker wrote what he thought might be his last letter to his sister, ending, "The grand attack is to take place to-morrow. I fear there will be great loss of life as the enemy are very strong. Good-night, the lights are being put out. I will finish this after the battle if I survive."[25]

The mortars on the raft fired the first shots of the battle for Mohammerah at dawn on 26th March. Their presence was quite unsuspected by the Persians, and the first shot burst on the parapet of the northern battery, wounding the Persian Brigadier and ten others, then at their morning prayers within the fort.[26] The shots were the signal for the warships of the British Squadron, which had already got up steam, to move into action. At about six o'clock in the morning they were within range of the forts, and anchoring in line ahead

MOHAMMERAH 26 MARCH 1857

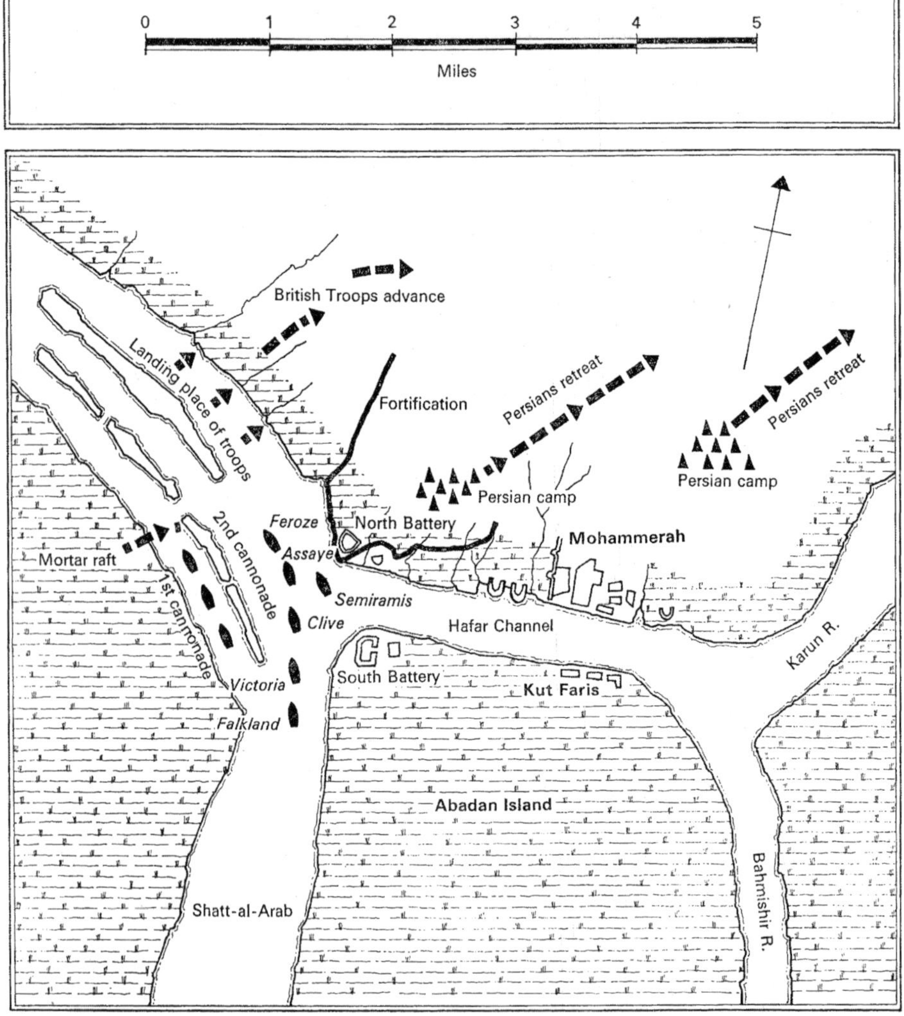

they opened fire. "The enemy's batteries opened along the whole line of defence, and with considerable effect on the hulls and rigging. The roar of the guns was tremendous, and the shells could be seen bursting in and among the defences in all directions. Many Arabs at first were seen sitting on the Turkish banks, coolly smoking, and watching the proceedings; but some Persian shot flying over the ships, and lodging in the bank close to them, soon sent them off."[27] After a heavy cannonade of more than an hour, at 7.45 the ships were ordered by the Commodore to close with the enemy, and moved in towards the forts. When they were close to the forts the attacking ships anchored, all except the *Assaye* which was too long (she was 280 feet) to profit from anchoring. Her Commander Adams handled her with very great skill, steaming up to the upstream angle of the northern fort at less than sixty yards' range, and then allowing her to drop downstream, firing the while: this manœuvre of steaming ahead and dropping back he continued for the whole of the action.[28] The two sloops set sail in order to come closer to the enemy, and all the gunners, including the heroic men on the mortar raft who were now having a hot time of it, fired as quickly as possible.*

The scene drawn and described by Captain Hunt of the 78th Highlanders, who was on board *Berenice*, seems to belong to another world, a world where war was a game fought with toy ships and men. The steam frigates were paddle steamers and in Captain Hunt's picture the tops of the paddle boxes of the nearest frigate can be seen crowded with tiny figures (see page 147). The morning was very

* The raft was commanded by Captain Worgan, of the Artillery, who was recommended for a V.C. for his part in this action. It was not awarded.

clear, with just enough wind to prevent the smoke from collecting. The ships, flags flying from every masthead, seemed decked for a holiday; the river glittered in the early sunlight, lined by its dark date-fringed banks. Through the grey fleecy cloud of smoke the sulky-looking batteries could just be seen.[29] The Indian Navy was attacking in broad daylight heavily defended positions, and to protect the men the upper decks were reinforced with "trusses of pressed hay round and upon the bulwarks."[30] The *Feroze* was later found to have 300 bullets buried in her sides, and vast numbers were shaken out of the hay trusses. For about three hours the ships and the forts fired on each other, while the transports remained at their anchorage.

The heavy British guns did a great deal of damage to the forts and the surrounding date-palms (one of the few photographs surviving from the campaigns shows the effect of the shot on the trees) and one after another the Persian guns fell silent. The able commander of the North Battery had been wounded by the first shot from the raft, and this took some of the enthusiasm from the defence. After three hours the Commodore of the attacking force, Rennie, decided that the forts were sufficiently subdued, and hoisted the signal ordering the light flotilla carrying the troops to advance past the forts and up the river to the disembarkation point. To make sure that he did not run aground, the captain of the leading vessel led the flotilla *inside* the frigates, between the lines of the battle. The *Berenice*, with General Havelock and the 78th Highlanders (including Captain Hunt and Lieutenant Barker) sailed under the guns of the fort, which were still being fired. The decks were so crowded with soldiers that there was hardly standing-room on board, and for a few minutes the men were helpless, crowded together like cattle in a pen within 100 yards of the Persian battery. But though the rigging was cut, and the hull of the ship struck several times, the decks escaped. The sailors on the frigates cheered loudly as each load of redcoats sailed past them.[31]

The disembarkation point was some hundred yards above the north battery. The landing was almost unopposed, and after some hours, delayed as before by the lack of small boats, most of the troops were on shore. One of the transports, the *Golden Era*, slung her horses on to the bank from the deck, and a detachment of forty-five Sind Horse was landed in half an hour by the expedient of throwing hay bales and mud into the water to make a platform.[32] The *Berenice* landed all the Highlanders by a plank. The rising tide filled the creeks as the landing continued, and made the ground impassable for the Horse Artillery and the Dragoons, so without these troops the general advanced through the date groves to where the main Persian army waited. Meanwhile the battered forts were occupied by the sailors.

The troops having been somewhat disorganised by the broken ground, the creeks and the date palms, as soon as the enemy came clearly in sight a halt was called, so that the lines of battle might be properly arranged. The battalions then marched onwards, greatly outnumbered and out-flanked by the Persians. But as the British advanced, so did the Persians vanish like a dream, so that when the invaders reached the lines only the deserted tents showed that this had indeed been the camp of an army.

The soldiers were, according to their chroniclers, disappointed that there was no fighting. But the amount of loot left behind was tremendous, even the men's dinners were lying ready to be eaten, and every tent was left standing, including that of the prince commanding. In the prince's tent was found a half-written despatch announcing "the glorious victory obtained by his army over the British, and how he had driven them into the sea, capturing their ships etc."[33] Of the sixteen guns captured there, one was cast at St. Petersburg and bore a Persian inscription about its presentation by the Czar in 1828. Nothing for the men, complained Corporal Borthwick, "No loot for us as men was warned the first catched would be tried by a General Court Martial. So we had not any chance of a bit carpet itself or anything else it is a damd poor Country."[34]

The unfortunate victors were not allowed to relax, but were hurried after the retreating Persians. The chase was unsuccessful, and after only three or four miles darkness closed in and the soldiers bivouacked in their line of battle. The night was bitterly cold, and the officers and men had no covering of any kind. Amidst the nervousness of camping in an unknown land close to an undefeated enemy two of the pickets fired on each other, wounding five men – the whole British casualties of the battle had only been forty-one. The Persians lost about 300 men and nearly all their baggage. The next day the British marched back to the former Persian camp by Mohammerah and thereafter lived in somewhat greater comfort, only suffering "from the swarms of flies under the trees by day, and from the myriads of fleas in the sand by night".[35]

*

Mohammerah was the last battle of the war. The Persian Army continued to retreat up river, as Outram sent after them three steamers and a force of 300 men under Captain Hunt, being the 5th Company and the Light Company of the 78th and 100 men from the 64th. The Persians, camped at Ahwaz on the Karun, saw the 300 men appearing from the jungle, trying to look like three regiments, and they took them for the advance guard of Outram's army. It was April Fool's Day. A fortunate shell from a gunboat landed beside the Persian H.Q., and killed two horses pulling the C.-in-C.'s green carriage; instantly he withdrew again, setting his army of 9,000 to 10,000 men off on another weary march, a hundred miles to Shuster, and by this time short of ammunition and food.[36] Corporal Borthwick (of the 5th Company) thought it lucky that his company and the 64th had been there, else "their would be no living with the Light Troops" after their rout of an army.[37]

The Ahwaz expedition returned to Mohammerah on 4th April, and within an hour of their return news came that peace had been signed and the war was over. The Persian commander, alarmed lest his army should be further pursued, sent a messenger to Outram, asking whether he was aware of the peace – Sir James replied "that, had he not been aware of it, he should have been at Shuster to beat his quarters up days before."[38] This rude answer expressed the disgust of the whole army at the peace just when, they felt, they were doing so well. They were disappointed at the close of what was, for them, a chance for prize money, promotion and glory. Outram wrote to Murray: "The previous official announcement of peace, received here on the night of 4th April, of course, tied our hands, and saved the Prince's army from unconditional capitulation." Havelock (who was told of the peace on his birthday, a Sunday morning when he had drawn up his troops for church parade) wrote to his wife: "So end my hopes of advantage from this war . . . It was to improve my claim [to promotion] that I faced every risk & promptly answered the invitation of the Bombay Government to come on this service. It has ended in smoke."[39]

The reputation of the Persian Army was not improved by the battles they had engaged in. The Shah ordered the fleet-footed officers of Mohammerah to be publicly disgraced, dragged along the ranks by rings through their noses, beaten and imprisoned. Their General, however, presented £8,000 to the Sadr Azim, and so was rewarded, for the same battle, with a sword and a robe of honour.[40]

The peace which was announced to Outram on 4th April had actually been signed in Paris on 4th March, before Stalker's death and before Ethersey's death, before even the first ships had set out for Mohammerah. Negotiations for peace had been going on since the war began, but it had not been easy to settle the matters in dispute.

CHAPTER EIGHT

Peace

MURRAY had of course, been in touch with the Foreign Office during the final stages of his quarrel with the Sadr Azim. The Cabinet, headed by Lord Palmerston, received his bulletins despondently and did not know quite what to do. In December, 1855, the Foreign Secretary wrote to his wife: "Altogether things are gloomy to-day, and that ass Murray seems to have got up a quarrel with Persia."[1] In January, 1856, another member of the Cabinet, Lord Granville, wrote to Canning: "We had a Cabinet today. The despatches from Ch. Murray have arrived, so voluminous that no one but Hammond has yet read them. Vernon Smith [in charge of Indian Affairs in the Cabinet] says that Murray's letters to the Shah are singularly offensive. His demands are quite absurd; yet orders are to be sent to occupy the island whose name I forget in the Persian Sea. G. Lewis and I objected, but were overruled."[2]

The Persians still seemed to want peace when Murray left Teheran. How much in earnest they were no one knew, but to the end of his life Murray believed that a stiff letter from the Foreign Office would have brought all the appropriate Persian apologies to himself. But there was instead of a stiff letter a long and fatal delay whilst the breach widened, Herat was attacked, and the unnecessary war began.

The first offer to negotiate was made by a Persian envoy

to the British Ambassador Lord Stratford de Redcliffe* at Constantinople. The meeting came to an unprofitable end, it is said because the British Ambassador refused, as a matter of protocol, to allow the Persian to use a chair *with arms* at the interview.[3]

Another envoy was sent, this time a man of much greater standing, a relative of the Shah called Ferukh Khan. There seems to have been no quarrel over protocol this time, but the demands of the British were so excessive that there was little chance of a settlement. Indeed it is difficult to believe that the Foreign Secretary who sent the instructions to Lord Stratford really wanted a settlement. The ambassador was instructed to ask the Persians to renounce all claims to Herat and to pay compensation to the Heratis; to give up part of their territory (Bunder Abbas) to a British ally, the Imam of Muscat; to make a new treaty with Britain allowing consuls in certain Persian cities; to satisfy the demands of all British subjects immediately; to receive Charles Murray with certain ceremonies and honours; and to dismiss the Sadr Azim. These demands were considered pretty steep even by the British, and the last impossible: it was said that they were not officially recorded in writing, so that they could not be called into question in Parliament.[4] How could any envoy possibly promise the dismissal of the prime minister of his country? In Persia it would probably cost him his head.

Considerable pressure was brought to bear upon Ferukh Khan in Constantinople, and he did eventually with the consent of his government agree to all demands except the dismissal of the Sadr Azim. The ceremonials to soothe

* Lord Canning's cousin, Stratford Canning, was created Viscount Stratford de Redcliffe in 1852. He was a very independent and rather difficult ambassador, nicknamed "The Great Elchi".

Murray were agreed upon "from the rank of the nobleman who was to receive him as his august foot crossed the frontier to the number of heaps of sugar and sweetmeats which were to be offered to him when he entered Teheran."[5] But all the negotiations took time, and meanwhile the British Fleet had sailed for Bushire. When the war actually began Ferukh Khan left Constantinople for Paris.

The proclamation declaring war on Persia which Lord Canning had published in Calcutta on 1st November, 1856, was not published in London until 16th December. News of the war was greeted in England with a mixture of disgust and derision, and with anti-war demonstrations in Bradford and Newcastle. But very little was ever known about the war in England because the government steadily refused to allow it to be discussed in Parliament. In the leisurely England of the 1850s, Parliament did not meet very often or for very long. And in this year of 1856-7 "the mingled listlessness and restlessness of the Session of 1856 required a vacation of unusual length, in order to replace the *stamina* which the Government had spent . . ."[6] Parliament had gone into recess in July, and Palmerston did not disturb even the members of the Cabinet until November, when they all came up from the country to London for the Lord Mayor's Dinner. During this interval there had been disputes with the United States, New Granada, Persia, Mexico, Naples, Russia, France and China – but the Cabinet had not met. War was declared on Persia, the Cabinet met, Christmas came and went, but it was not until 3rd February, 1857, six months after the summer recess, that Parliament opened. By this time the Opposition was very angry, and the government apprehensive. The Foreign Secretary wrote to his wife on the eve of the opening of Parliament: "The Cabinet of course was unpunctual – no operation so long as that of criticising and amending a Queen's speech. Persia, Naples and China stand in awful array next to each other, and will of course give rise to never-ending debates."[7] The next day the Queen's speech was dominated by the foreign troubles surrounding the government and home policy took a very second place.

As soon as the speech was debated, Palmerston's policy, particularly in respect to the Chinese and Persian wars was attacked fiercely in both houses. Both wars (the Chinese War was said by its opponents to be fought to ensure the British right to sell opium to the Chinese against the Chinese Government's wishes) were called unjust, unnecessary, bullying, badly planned and badly executed.* The Opposition maintained that Parliament should have been recalled at the beginning of the Persian War – Disraeli opening his attack with "I confess that I was somewhat surprised when I heard of the Persian War . . .'[8] The Opposition was particularly anxious to know by whose authority the War had been started, and who was going to pay for it, India or England.

The government fought an ingenious rearguard action, asking the House not to consider the war until papers relating to it were laid before the House: and refusing to produce the papers firstly because peace negotiations were under way, and finally because the Peace Treaty had not been ratified by the Persians. And so, as Mr Roebuck

* Members of the government too had disliked the Persian war, although it was their duty to defend it. Granville's view was expressed to Canning "the war was a great scrape . . . I have great doubts whether it is the best policy to treat Orientals in a way inconsistent with all the principles of justice . . ." (Fitzmaurice, *Granville*, I, 225.)

pointed out in the House of Commons in February, 1857, the position of the House was farcical. "War is declared, and of that war the House of Commons knows nothing. War has been carried on, and of the mode of its prosecution we are in total ignorance. We are told that negotiations are now in progress. Of their nature this House knows nothing . . . if we put in a question before hostilities take place, we are told that we are too soon; if while they are in progress, we are told that we are inter-meddling; and if after they have come to a termination, we then are told we are too late."[9] Without the relevant papers it was very difficult for the Opposition to attack the government, and by the time the papers were produced the war was over and a matter of history. In the event there was never a major debate on the Persian War, because the government was defeated over the China War. At the General Election, Palmerston was returned with a greatly increased majority and could afford to ignore criticisms of the Persian War.

While Parliament was in session, Ferukh Khan, the Persian Ambassador and plenipotentiary, was crossing Europe from Constantinople in search of peace. He was fêted in London, whilst news of the British victories in Persia were arriving in England.[10] Soon after he left for Paris, where he was to be ambassador to the Emperor Napoleon III. He was a popular and exotic figure at the Tuileries, where he wore a green tunic, crossed by a blue ribbon, a cashmere pelisse lined with fur and studded with diamonds, a sword and belt also studded with jewels, and round his neck a portrait of his Shah, set in diamonds.[11]

Ferukh Khan had full powers to negotiate with Britain, and between the social activities of the Paris season he discussed peace with Lord Cowley. In March, 1857, agreement was nearly reached – but Palmerston's Government was fast approaching defeat in the House of Commons and Ferukh Khan in Paris was urged by his friends in London to postpone signature of the treaty until the government fell, in the hopes of better terms from a new government.[12] However the Persians were afraid that any delay would bring fresh military disasters in Persia. Early in the morning of 4th March, Palmerston's Government was defeated (and resigned) over the China War: the same day the settlement with Persia was announced.

By the terms of the treaty of peace[13] the Shah agreed to withdraw his troops from Herat, and to relinquish all claims to sovereignty over it. He also agreed not to interfere with the internal affairs of Afghanistan, and to recognise the independence of Herat. All prisoners taken at Herat were to be set free without ransom. The British Mission was to be received at Teheran with apologies, and special apologies were to be made to Mr Murray. The slave trade was to be suppressed in the Persian Gulf (this clause, dear to the British public, had nothing to do with the war). The British, on the other hand, agreed that in future they would not protect Persians not actually in their employ. Nothing was said about Bunder Abbas or the Sadr Azim. The terms now agreed to were less severe than those offered by the Persians and refused by Britain at Constantinople before ever the war began.

Outram had been in his tent at Mohammerah, asleep, when the news came to him that peace had been agreed in Paris a month before. He was annoyed that peace had been made while he was doing so well, but one part of the peace agreement he found particularly irritating, and even dangerous. The Shah had been given three months in which to ratify the Treaty – three months in which Outram could make no offensive move, at the end of which time the Shah might find some reason for not complying with Britain's demands. If the Shah waited until the full term had elapsed it would then be June, the hot and deadly season, when the troops in the Gulf would begin to sicken and die. Nevertheless to withdraw the troops to a healthier station would tempt the Shah to repudiate the treaty, and if he did so it would be too late in the season to begin a new campaign.

The soldiers and N.C.O.s were, strangely, not told of the peace. Eight days later Corporal Borthwick was still guessing as to his future – but, intelligent man, he noticed that instead of fifty rounds of ammunition each man had only twenty rounds "so it is a pretty shure sign of peace."[14]

Outram prepared to make the best of it, and planned an encampment at Mohammerah. There were to be mud huts for the troops (made of date trees, mud and river water) which were to have camel thorn screens over the doors and windows, constantly damped (with river water) to keep some coolness in the huts.[15] The officers were told to get what they could for themselves – which was nothing, according to Lieutenant Barker. Some were burrowing into the earth like rabbits, thinking it would be cooler down there – but then no one knew how high the river would rise.[16] Outram applied for material to supply the whole force with gauze curtains as "all the natives consulted . . . declare that for several months, beginning with the present, sleep will be out of the question, owing to the swarms of mosquitoes, unless our men are properly screened from their virulent attacks."[17] He also applied for books, newspapers, games, etc., to entertain the men in the huts. By 23rd April (if not earlier) there was a special letter frank at Mohammerah "FIELD FORCE PERSIA".[18]

Colonel Jacob was very opposed to the idea of keeping the troops at Mohammerah, and wrote to Outram with the frankness that can hardly have endeared him to his superiors: "I am quite certain that if you do as you propose, you will make a most shocking mess of it, and perhaps cause the most serious loss by sickness."[19] Already many of the soldiers were being sick after meals, especially after breakfast, and subsequently one third of the officers of the 78th Highlanders alone developed jaundice.[20] The very air seemed full of sickness and death.

Fortunately the situation changed, and Outram's mud huts were never used. At the end of April he returned to Bushire, and found that the difficulties of getting building materials and workmen there were so great that most of the European troops would be still in tents when the fierce heat began.[21] He also received alarming news about the restless spirit of the Bengal Army, and the great need for European troops in India. On his own initiative therefore, and with the help of a vague directive from Bombay, Outram withdrew all the troops from Mohammerah, none too soon in their opinion for the temperature was already 104°F. in their tents and likely to go to 140°F.[22] Two sloops of war were left in the roads at Mohammerah, and nearly all the European troops in the force were sent back to India. Outram was also trying to dispose of the baggage animals originally collected for the advance up-river from Mohammerah, now an embarrassment to guard and feed. There were 5,000 camels and 1,000 mules, and many of Outram's letters ended with such plaintive notes as "P.S. Would you now wish any mules to be sent . . . we have 500 splendid animals on board."[23]

Lord Dunkellin had already returned to India, strangely enough on 1st April, exactly a year after he had left for Persia. His C.-in-C. wrote: "his departure was regretted by the whole army, for he was a general favourite, and I am sure would have distinguished himself highly had the enemy been more worthy to contend with British soldiers."[24] Most of the senior officers were now anxious to return to India. John Jacob, who had never really wanted to go to Persia, was increasingly restless at Bushire where he had not seen any of the action of the war. He was angry at the treatment of the Sind Horse, which had spent a good deal of time sailing up and down the Gulf obeying Outram's contradictory orders. There was a typical incident at the end of April: part of the Sind Horse came into Bushire harbour, sent down from Mohammerah – but at the same time another ship sailed in bringing Outram's orders to return the troops to Mohammerah. Jacob obeyed the orders, but pointed out that the continued movement by sea was ruining the horses and breaking the officers' hearts.

At this time, too, when Jacob was sick with diarrhoea, Outram himself arrived at Bushire, and suggested a reorganisation of the force, leaving John Jacob with a Brigade only. Jacob was furious and replied: "As for myself, I would consent to serve as a private soldier if you wished it, *and I felt that by so doing I could be advancing good work*, but you can hardly, I think, be serious in proposing to leave me here under command of General Havelock, to look after some sowars* at Halilah Bay or elsewhere." He asked to be allowed to return to his post in India which he had never

* Native cavalrymen.

wanted to leave, and added: "From what I have heard since I last wrote to you (from very many persons whom I can rely on) I should feel that serving under General H at all was moral DEATH . . ."[25] Nevertheless Jacob was persuaded to remain in charge of the troops at Bushire, being given the whole command whilst Havelock returned to India. Outram considered his presence more important than the retention of a whole regiment of Europeans, and wrote to the Governor-General: "All ranks, officers or men, white faces or black, regard General Jacob with equal devotion; and his influence with troops is such as I have never seen surpassed . . ."[26]

Sailing back from Bushire to Mohammerah, Outram had a sad mishap. About 11 p.m. when all were sound asleep and the steamer going full speed ahead, she ran heavily aground. The ship being towed (there always seemed to be a tow, owing to the shortage of steamers) drawing less water crashed into the steamer and the whole of the stern cabin was carried away. Outram was buried in the debris and hauled out through a hole, bruised and with a black eye and broken nose. The two ships remained interlocked for nine hours. An officer on Jacob's staff who was there and drew a sketch of the ships for Jacob wrote: "I never laughed so much in my life."[27] The pain of Outram's nose was assuaged by the news that the Shah had after all, ratified the treaty well within the time limit. Mohammerah could now be safely left, and a mere skeleton force left at Bushire until Herat was evacuated. Havelock was reported "rather grumpy" at losing his command, and his staff likewise.

On 15th May, the British guard was withdrawn from Mohammerah and the town, which had become an embarrassment, was handed over to Sheikh Jahir, leader of part of the Cha'ab tribe, to administer.[28] It was difficult to know quite what to do with Mohammerah as it was claimed by Turkey, by Persia and by two of the Cha'ab Sheikhs, who were quite willing to hold it from either Turkey or Persia. So as a British compromise the town was given to Sheikh Jahir, but at the same time the Persian Governor of the province was invited to send a deputy to administer the town.

Outram sailed up river to Baghdad, to confer with Charles Murray about the Mission to see Herat evacuated, and found time to bombard the Government of India, the Government of Bombay and John Company's directors with lists of officers and men deserving rewards, pensions, promotions, medals, special notice, even benefices in England. He made numerous recommendations for the Victoria Cross, instituted during the Crimean War and then as now the most coveted decoration in the British Army. Three men were recommended for the V.C. for their part in the taking of Reshire and one for his part at Mohammerah (Captain Worgan, commander of the mortar battery). No less than fifteen were recommended for the battle of Khoosh-ab (including Cornet Combe) and as the lower ranks of the cavalry all did heroically, Outram suggested that two Crosses be given to each troop.[29] In its early days the Victoria Cross was somewhat more easily won, but nevertheless Outram had overdone his recommendations considerably. Eventually three awards were made, a Victoria Cross to Captain J. A. Wood, 20th Bombay Native Infantry, for his part in the taking of Reshire, and a Cross each to Lieutenant J. G. Malcolmson and Lieutenant and Adjutant A. T. Moore for the charge of the 3rd Bombay Light Cavalry at Khoosh-ab.[30] Outram himself was given a

G.C.B. and the Government of India thankfully decided that as Stalker was dead, Leeke need not be given anything. A clasp for *Persia* was added to the appropriate India General Service Medal, and battle honours of *Persia, Reshire, Koosh-ab* and later *Bushire* were awarded to the regiments that had taken part in the campaign.*[31]

In Baghdad, Outram kept remembering other people he had forgotten to commend and sending further letters to the government – no less than twenty-seven letters in his book[32] are about specific rewards of one kind or another, and many have postscripts adding further names. As a result the Government of India, with some annoyance, had to keep issuing extra notifications.

*

Henry Havelock had returned to India, arriving on 29th May, 1857, "to receive the astounding intelligence that the Native Regiments had mutinied at Meerut, & that the Fortress of Delhi was in the hands of the mutineers, whilst disaffection seemed everywhere spreading in the Upper Provinces."[33] Outram was still in Baghdad when he heard on 7th June from Karachi that there was mutiny in Bengal and "the native troops of the Bengal Army [were] in insurrection from Delhi and upwards . . . at Delhi, Europeans had been massacred."[34] Or, as Dunkellin put it, "The General commanding at Meerut, Hewitt by name, but generally known as Bloody Bill, allowed the coach to be upset . . ."[35] Outram was extremely distressed, as his wife

* These must be some of the easiest battle-honours ever won. At Reshire the action was little more than a skirmish: at Khoosh-ab only the cavalry were engaged, and that for a short time: at Bushire the soldiers were not in contact with the enemy at all.

and son were thought to be in Delhi, and it was four days before he heard that they were safe. On hearing of the Mutiny, Outram, that strange contradictory man, came alive again. He saw at once that all the troops England could furnish would be needed in India, suggested that the force then on its way to attack China would be diverted, and suggested to Lord Stratford de Redcliffe that he obtain permission for troops from England to be sent overland through Egypt. The general at once left Baghdad for Bushire, where he found a telegram from Lord Canning telling him and Jacob to return to India immediately as "we want all our best men here."[36] The red tide of the Mutiny swept over India, destroying as it went many things, including John Company's rule. When the Mutiny was over, the Company's power had gone for ever, and Queen Victoria became an empress.

So Outram went back to India, to Calcutta and to Lucknow, to great fame and a seat on the Governor-General's Council and a grave in Westminster Abbey. But he decided that poor Jacob should stay at Bushire, in charge of the garrison of about 5,000 men (including Lieutenant Brown, 20th Native Infantry) guarded by a steam frigate, because Outram feared that the Shah might take the chance of breaking the treaty. Jacob was to remain at Bushire until word came that Herat was evacuated and the former dynasty re-established.

Murray returned to Teheran in July, and all the proper apologies were made. The Shah and the Sadr Azim made much of him, and anyone but Murray might have thought it overdone. Exclaiming continually how much they liked Mr Murray, they even offered the Indian Government 30,000 soldiers to quell the Mutiny, at the same time boasting that while the war had been going on they themselves had been fomenting the conspiracy among the Mohammedan princes in India. *Now* however, they only wanted to help restore order.[37] None of the Sadr Azim's letters to the princes are known to have survived, and the responses of the princes are unknown. Although it was alleged at the King of Delhi's trial after the Mutiny that he had conspired with the Shah, this was never proved, and Sir John Lawrence disbelieved it: after all, if the Shah had been involved in a plot to raise rebellion in India, he would hardly have made peace in May, 1857, the month when the British were in greatest danger of being driven out of India.[38]

What was the fate of the Hashims and Herat? The Hashims had made their peace with the Persian Government a long time before, before ever the British arrived in the Gulf, and "Mrs Hashim" had been released from prison and the Mirza given employment by the Persian Government.

Outram and Murray had despatched Lieutenant-Colonel Taylor to Herat to see that the evacuation was properly carried out. Colonel Robert Lewis Taylor, C.B., who had been on Murray's staff at Teheran (see page 46) and had been Outram's political secretary and head of intelligence, was probably a bad choice. Outram's military secretary Malcolm Green was asked to go to Herat but his brother wrote to Jacob: "I have strongly advised him that unless he can be perfectly independent of Mr Murray to have nothing to do with it. Mr Murray is a snob, is hated and detested throughout the land and any man who has anything to do with him will be associated in his acts. Major Taylor is a tool of his brought up in the same school."[39] Taylor was sent off, as Murray had been in 1855, without any of the customary presents for the ruler he was visiting, and he was not greeted with great joy – indeed he was hardly greeted at all, for he camped outside the city of Herat and sent, one after another, three messengers inside the city walls. None of them returned.[40]

The Governor of Herat was now Sultan Ahmed Khan (also called Sultan Jan), for the Persians had taken the precaution of murdering the ruler of 1856, Mohammed Yusuf, who was hacked to pieces in Teheran when the Persians heard that a clause of the peace treaty would deal with the release of prisoners of war.[41] Ahmed Khan was in Teheran at the time, and left two days later for Herat, after no doubt coming to some arrangement with the Sadr Azim. He was anxious to reach Herat as soon as possible, and succeeded all too well, for he reached the city before any orders had been received about him from the Shah. He hurried in to see the temporary Governor of Herat (appointed by the Shah on his capture of the city) but he was asleep, and when the sentries refused him admission, Ahmed Khan in a rage stabbed one of them. The temporary governor, hearing that an Afghan had wounded a sentry and tried to force himself into his presence, had Ahmed Khan severely beaten. Later in the day orders came that Ahmed Khan was to be made Prince of Herat.[42] He was the son-in-law of Dost Mohammed Khan (Ahmed's favourite wife was the Dost's favourite daughter) but the two men were not on good terms.

In time the new Prince of Herat did agree to see Colonel Taylor, and he was in October, 1857, given a brilliant reception. He found the city in a most miserable state, without artillery, muskets or ammunition, with battered defences and derelict houses. The Heratis felt they had lost face, and hated the Persians for the humiliation of their defeat as well as for the cruelties of the occupation.

For the time being the Heratis were very Anglophile. They desperately needed some protection and some aid, and hoped that India would provide all, as she had done after the 1838 siege. The ruler wore English tailored trousers and coat, English boots or shoes, rode on an English saddle and knew a few words of English in addition to the military words of command which were all English.[43] Colonel Taylor recommended that money and arms be given to Herat. But the Government of India was totally immersed in its own troubles (the Mutiny was followed by an acute financial crisis) and nothing was done. The Persians however lavished money on Herat and soon the prince was very pro-Persian and anti-English. What with one thing and another, Taylor found his position so embarrassing that, like all the British Chiefs of Mission to Herat, he was obliged in February, 1858, to withdraw very hurriedly indeed.

Before he went he abetted Murray in almost the last act of Murray's Teheran Mission, the last and most awful blunder. It is clear from Lord Canning's secret papers that Murray either originated or was deeply involved in a plot to dethrone the Prince of Herat and replace him with one thought to be more amenable. There is no record to show if the Foreign Office had foreknowledge of Murray's plot, or if he thought it all up on his own. It was hatched in Teheran, and (of course) the Sadr Azim found out all about it. It was (of course) a failure. The unsuccessful pretender Mohammed Reza thereafter lived a wandering life in disguise, carrying with him like a talisman a paper which caused a shudder in Calcutta and London, a paper committing the British Government to his support. The pretender's family con-

The charge of the 3rd Bombay Light Cavalry at the battle of Khoosh-ab

Mohammerah in 1857: (top) Northern half (below) Southern half

The Indian Navy attacks the forts of Mohammerah

The morning after the battle of Mohammerah, interior of the northern fort

After the battle of Mohammerah. The gun battery on Hafar creek with the northern battery in the background

stantly asked for money to make up for the hardships and dangers to which they had been exposed in trying to carry out the views of the British Government.[44] It is hardly surprising that Taylor was forced to withdraw. The ruler of Herat knew all about the plot, as the Sadr Azim had kept him informed from Teheran, and as the investigator of the failure wrote to the Foreign Secretary, "Sultan Ahmed Khan appears to have been fully informed at the time of all particulars of the transaction, Your Lordship can hardly be surprised at the mistrust of the English and disposition to rely on Russo-Persian support, which have ever since marked his policy."[45]

So Taylor left Herat to its own fate, which was to remain pro-Persian until 1862, when Ahmed Khan combined with the Persians and marched against Kandahar. Dost Mohammed Khan called for British aid, and on 26th May, 1863, having repulsed the Persians and Ahmed Khan, the old man achieved his life-long ambition and captured Herat, dying a few days later.[46] Ever since that day Herat and the territory round about the city have been part of Afghanistan, the kingdom forged by Dost Mohammed Khan. He was buried near Herat.

Charles Murray went home to England in 1857, taking a year's sick leave, and no doubt the Foreign Office and the Government of India were relieved to know he was out of Persia. He was subsequently appointed to Saxony, Copenhagen and Lisbon, became a K.C.B. and married a second time. He died in his ninetieth year, finding his diplomatic career a disappointing one after all.

All through the hot weather of 1857, Jacob remained in command at Bushire while northern India was ablaze with mutiny. It was not until October, 1857, that the remainder of the force was withdrawn and by the time it reached India the worst of the Mutiny was over. Less than a week before the last men left Persia a macabre incident happened. Two Persians tried to dig up General Stalker's grave, looking for treasure they supposed to have been buried with the general. According to one of the robbers, "the General Sahib arose and smote him a violent blow on the head, on which the tomb immediately fell and crushed him."[47]

Jacob was one of the last to leave Bushire. He wrote in his diary: "2nd October. Embarked this morning on board of the *Charles Grant* and sailed for Kurrachee towed by the *Feroze* and with a flat towed astern of us. Fair wind passed three ships going to Bombay."[48]

Captain Felix Jones was left alone again at Bushire, as he had been before the war. His policemen with their wooden truncheons and the moral force of Jones in his armchair at home were sufficient to keep the peace: but he was lonely, he wrote to Jacob. The shouting and the tumult had died, the captains had departed, and each week seemed like a year.[49]

Epilogue

So ended John Company's last war. For the red ruin of mutiny which whirled through Bengal swept away the East India Company, the Company's Army, the Indian Navy and much else besides. When the Mutiny was over, John Company's day was over too, and Queen Victoria became an Empress and India an Empire for nearly a hundred years. The Persian War was forgotten in the holocaust that came after it. It had been a successful campaign, in that it achieved its limited objects, of restoring Mr Murray with honour to Teheran, and persuading the Shah to leave Herat alone for a time. But these might have been achieved, as Murray complained, at the price of a stiff despatch from the Foreign Secretary, and the same or better terms could have been agreed at Constantinople before the war began. The Persians were surprised at the mildness of the British who asked for no indemnity, took no land, but merely restored the *status quo*. The Heratis coined a new proverb, based on their experience of 1838, 1852 and 1856: "Herat never submits to Persia so long as there is grain in the fort: and it then only submits until the English take Bushire."

The operations of the war seem to have been successful in spite of the incompetence of most of the military leaders, because the Persians were so much more incompetent. Persia was humiliated by the war and further weakened for the advance of Russia. For the British, peace came only just in time for the regiments and the generals to take part in the Mutiny campaigns.

Old Herat remained unchanged for a century, its narrow lanes and crowded bazaars hidden behind the massive walls, honeycombed with diggings. Britain again considered war to protect the city many times in the years to come, especially in 1885. Outside the walls a new city grew up, rather like Bournemouth, with wide avenues, modern shops and grand but empty hotels such as the "Parq Otel". In the 1950s the walls of Herat were taken down, leaving only the earthworks of the citadel, and now a large airport brings foreigners to the once fabled city.

The small port of Mohammerah turned out to be very important after all, for the island on which the south battery was built was called Abadan, and became an enormous oil refinery, at one time the largest in the world. The expedition had given it back to the Cha'ab Arabs, and it was for them even better than a gold mine.

What was the true cause of John Company's last war, which cost some two to three million pounds? Was it what would soon be called "Imperial strategy" or Mr Murray's princess? *The Times* had no doubt: "While the newspapers and correspondents and officials, with patriotic decorum, are assuming that Herat is the cause of the war, there is not a company in which it is not stated as a matter of notoriety that the real cause is that ridiculous quarrel over a Persian Lady . . . while the broadsheet at breakfast proceeds on the solemn supposition that it is all about Herat, the talk of the dinner table equally takes for granted that it is about a Persian courtier's runaway mistress or wife." The Parliamentary papers dealing with the Persian War were called simply "Affairs of Persia 1857."

Bibliography

MANUSCRIPT SOURCES

The Canning Papers

The papers of Charles John, 1st Earl Canning, Governor-General and Viceroy of India, 1856-62, are of the greatest importance in the study of the Persian War. It was the custom for the Governor-General to bring home with him from India large quantities of so-called "private" papers, and these deal with every facet of administration. In addition to these papers there are also preserved some papers of Canning before he went to India, and some papers and diaries of Lady Canning. Letters to the Cannings from Lord Dunkellin, their nephew, have been kept with the Indian papers. Lord Canning's Papers passed to the 2nd Marquess of Clanricarde, and from him to the 6th Earl of Harewood. They are now deposited at Leeds City Libraries Archives Department, at Sheepscar Library, Leeds. References such as "Canning Papers: Letters to Governor of Bombay" refer to these archives.

The Dalhousie Papers

James Andrew Broun, 10th Earl and 1st Marquess of Dalhousie, was Governor-General of India from 1848 to 1856, immediately before Lord Canning. He brought home from India a large number of "private" papers, which are now deposited at the Scottish Record Office, Register House, Edinburgh. Both the Hon. C. A. Murray and Sir James Outram continued to correspond with Lord Dalhousie after his return to Scotland in 1856. The photographs of Mohammerah in this book are preserved amongst Lord Dalhousie's papers, but unfortunately there is no indication as to the photographer's identity. They are interesting because of their very early date for war photographs.

The Elphinstone Papers

John, 13th Lord Elphinstone, was Governor of Madras, 1837-42 and Governor of Bombay, 1853-60. His papers were (together with those of other members of his family who had worked in India) deposited in the India Office Library in 1957 on permanent loan (MSS Eur. F 87). As Governor of the Presidency which supplied troops, etc., for the Persian War, Elphinstone's Papers contain many details not found elsewhere.

The Outram Papers

Sir James Outram, Commander of the Persian Force in succession to General Stalker, was a prolific correspondent. His papers are preserved at the National Army Museum, now being moved from Camberley to Chelsea.

The Havelock Papers

Sir Henry Havelock's Papers are part of the archives of the Havelock-Allan family, found at Blackwell Grange, Darlington, and now in the North Riding Record Office, Northallerton, Yorkshire. Unfortunately Sir Henry was not a very interesting letter-writer, and his papers do little more than confirm the main outline of events.

Jacob's Papers

John Jacob of Jacobabad, commander of the cavalry in Persia and later in charge of the garrison at Bushire, kept a diary intermittently during 1857. Most of the interesting parts of the diary – which was kept seldom – are printed by H. T. Lambrick in *John Jacob of Jacobabad*, 1960. Mr Lambrick, Oriel College, Oxford, owns the diary. Many of Jacob's papers are among the India Office Records or in the India Office Library.

Surgeon Mills' Diary

Surgeon John Mills was on the Persian Campaign from the beginning until May, 1857. He was in charge of the sappers' and staff medical care. He kept a daily diary, and the volumes covering the period are at the National Army Museum.

Lieutenant J. B. Hardy's Notebook

John Braithwaite Hardy, Bombay Artillery, served in the Persian Expedition. He was on the mortar raft commanded by Captain Worgan which shelled the Mohammerah forts. He was subsequently sent to Herat with Colonel Taylor. His notebook contains an account of his journeys in Persia and to Herat, illustrated with rough sketches of people and places. It is now in the National Army Museum.

Lieutenant F. W. Brown's Letters

Francis William Brown, Lieutenant 20th Bombay N.I., took part in the whole Persian Campaign from the landing at Halilah Bay to the final evacuation of Bushire. He wrote many letters to his family, especially to his sister, which are now in the National Library of Scotland.

Midshipman H. W. Estridge's Notes

Midshipman Henry Whatley Estridge of the sloop *Clive* recorded his part in the war from the day after the capture of Bushire to the end of the campaign. His notes are now in the National Maritime Museum, Greenwich (HIS/15).

Assistant Surgeon Sylvester's Diary

Assistant Surgeon John Henry Sylvester kept a diary in India from 1854 to 1861. He joined the Persian Expedition but arrived too late for any action. His diary belongs to Miss B. A. S. Hodder or Worthing, Sussex.

Cornet Combe's Letters

Charles Combe, cornet in the 3rd Bombay Light Cavalry, wrote a number of interesting letters to his family between 1856 and 1859. They were subsequently printed for private circulation only, and the letters can no longer be traced. I have not been able to see a copy of the book, but Cornet Combe's son, Mr. Edmond Combe of Richmond, Surrey, kindly lent me a typescript of the book.

Corporal John Borthwick's Letters

Corporal John Borthwick, 78th Highlanders, wrote to his wife at Poona during the Persian War. Some of his letters are now at the Regimental Museum of the Queen's Own Highlanders (Seaforth and Camerons), Fort George, Inverness.

India Office Records

The India Office records at 197 Blackfriars Road, London, contain official papers of the East India Company and the Board of Control, and of their legal successor, the India Office. Many papers amongst the India Office records touch on the Persian War, especially Political and Secret Department, Vol. 112 (Persia) 1857.

India Office Library

The India Office Library was created by the East India Company and continued to be used by the India Office. In 1947 both library and records were transferred to the Commonwealth Relations

Office. Many archives dealing with India and Pakistan have been deposited in the India Office Library, including (as well as those mentioned above) papers of Charles Masson and Lewis Pelly.

Public Record Office

Many volumes among the Foreign Office Records deal with Persian affairs during the period of Murray's Mission: F.O. 60/189-252 (1854-60), and F.O. 248/158-92. (*Lists and Indexes No. LII: List of Foreign Office Records to* 1878).

The Times
The Illustrated London News
The Saturday Review
The Edinburgh Review
Punch
The Spectator
Hansard
Foreign Office Blue Book Vol. LXIII (1857) *Affairs of Persia*

Anon	*Frontier and Overseas Expeditions from India.* 6 vols. (Vol. VI deals with the Persian War) 1911, Calcutta
Abbott, James	*From Heraut to Khiva.* 2 vols. 1856
Anglesey, Marquess of (ed.)	*Sergeant Pearman's Memoirs.* 1968
Baird, J. G. A. (ed.)	*Private Letters of the Marquess of Dalhousie.* 1910
Ballard, Lt.	"The Persian War of 1856-57," *Blackwood's Magazine*, Sept. 1861
Barker, Sir George Digby	*Letters from Persia and India, 1857-1859. A subaltern's experiences in war.* 1915

Bell, Mark S. — *An account of the British Wars with Persia from the Occupation of Kharaj in 1838 together with a Precis of Contemporaneous events and abstracts of Important correspondence connected with the War of 1856–57*. 1889, Simla

Bellew, Henry Walter — *Journal of a Political Mission to Afghanistan in 1857, under Major (now Colonel) Lumsden; with an Account of the Country and People*. 1862

Bond, Brian (ed.) — *Victorian Military Campaigns*. 1967

Burnes, Alexander — *Travels into Bokhara: being the account of a Journey from India to Cabool, Tartary, and Persia; also, narrative of a voyage on the Indus* (etc.). 3 vols. 1834

Burnes, Alexander — *Cabool: being a personal narrative of a journey to, and residence in that city in the years 1836, 7 and 8*. 1842

"Chambers' History" — See [Dodd, G.]

Conolly, Arthur — *Journey to the North of India, Overland from England through Russia, Persia and Affghaunistaun*. 2 vols. 1838

Cunningham, Sir H. S. — *Earl Canning*. 1891

Curzon, Hon. George N. — *Persia and the Persian Question*. 2 vols. 1892

Davidson, Hugh — *History & Services of the 78th Highlanders (Ross-shire Buffs) 1793–1881*. 2 vols. 1901

Davis, H. W. C. — "The Great Game in Asia," *Proc. of British Academy* XII (1926), 227–56

[Dodd, G.] — *History of the Indian revolt and expedition to Persia*. 1859 (Published anonymously as "Chambers' History")

Eastwick, E. B. — *Journal of a Diplomate's Three Years' Residence in Persia.* 2 vols. 1864

Ferrier, J. P. — *Caravan Journeys and Wanderings in Persia, Afghanistan, Turkistan, and Beloochistan; with Historical Notices of the Countries Lying Between Russia and India.* Translated by Capt. William Jesse. (With an appendix on the Herat Mission of 1838-41 by Sir John Login). 1856

Fitzmaurice, Lord Edmond — *The Life of Granville George Leveson Gower, Second Earl Granville K.G. 1815-1891.* 2 vols. 1905

Forbes, Archibald — *Havelock.* 1908

Forrest, George W. (ed.) — *Selection from the Travels and Journals Preserved in the Bombay Secretariat.* 1906, Bombay

Forster, George — *A Journey from Bengal to England, through the northern part of India, Kashmire, Afghanistan, and Persia,* etc. 2 vols. 1798, 1808

Fortescue, Sir J. W. — *A History of the British Army.* 13 vols. (Vol. XIII is the relevant one). 1930

Fraser, James B. — *A Journey into Khorasan.* 1825

Fraser-Tytler, Sir W. Kerr — *Afghanistan. A Study of Political Developments in Central Asia.* 1950

Gail, Marzieh — *Persia and the Victorians.* 1951

Gobineau, Comte Arthur de — *Trois Ans en Asie.* 2 vols. 1923, Paris

Goldsmid, Sir F. J. — *James Outram.* 2 vols. 1881

Gordon, L. L. — *British Battles and Medals.* 1962

Greaves, R. L. — *Persia and the Defence of India 1884-1892.* 1959

Gregory, Sir William	*An Autobiography*. 1894
Grey, C., and Garrett, H. L. O.	*European Adventurers of Northern India 1785 to 1849*. 1929, Lahore
Habberton, William	*Anglo-Russian Relations concerning Afghanistan*. 1937, Urbana U.S.A.
Hare, Augustus J. C.	*The Story of Two Noble Lives*. 3 vols. 1893
Holdich, Sir T. H.	*The Indian Borderland 1880–1900*. 1909
Hunt, G. H.	*Outram & Havelock's Persian Campaign*. 1858
Jacob, Brig.-Gen. John	*Letters on the Persian War and on the Frontier Arrangements of our Indian Empire*. Pamphlet, privately printed. 1857
Kaye, Sir John W.	*History of the War in Afghanistan*. 2 vols. 1851
Kaye, Sir John W.	*Lives of Indian officers*. 2 vols. 1867
Kaye, Sir John W.	*History of the Sepoy War*. 3 vols. 1880
Khan, The Aga	*World Enough and Time*. 1954
Kubie, Nora	*Road to Nineveh (The Adventures and Excavations of Sir Austen Henry Layard)*. 1965
Lal, Mohan	*Life of the Amir Dost Mohammed Khan of Kabul, with his Political Proceedings towards the English, Russian and Persian Governments. Including the Victories and Disasters of the British Army in Affghanistan*. 2 vols. 1846
Lal, Mohan	*Journal of a Tour through the Panjab, Afghanistan, Turkistan, Khorasan, and a Part of Persia, in Company with Lieut. Burnes and Dr. Gerard*. 1846

Lambrick, H. T.	*John Jacob of Jacobabad.* 1960
Lee-Warner, Sir W.	*The Marquis of Dalhousie.* 2 vols. 1904
Login, Lady L.	*Sir John Login and Duleep Singh.* 1890
Low, C. R.	*History of the Indian Navy (1613–1863).* 2 vols. 1877
MacDonald, Robert	*Personal narrative of military travel and adventure in Turkey and Persia.* 1859, Edinburgh
Maclagan, Michael	*Clemency Canning.* 1962
Maclean, Fitzroy	*A Person from England and other Travellers to Turkestan.* 1958
Macrory, Patrick	*Signal Catastrophe. The Story of the Disastrous Retreat from Kabul 1842.* 1966
Malleson, George Bruce	*Herat: The Granary and Garden of Central Asia.* 1880
Malmesbury, Earl of	*Memoirs of an ex-Minister.* 2 vols. 1884
Marsh, H. C.	*A ride through Islam, being a journey through Persia and Afghanistan to India, via Meshed, Herat and Kandahar.* 1877
Marshman, J. C.	*Memoirs of Major-General Sir Henry Havelock, K.C.B.* 1860
Martineau, John	*The Life and Correspondence of Sir Bartle Frere, Bart., G.C.B., F.R.S., etc.* 2 vols. 1895
Masson, Charles	*Narrative of Various Journeys in Balochistan, Afghanistan and the Panjab; Including a Residence in those Countries from 1826 to 1838.* 3 vols. 1842
Maxwell, Sir Herbert	*The Hon. Sir Charles Augustus Murray, K.C.B.* 1898
Maxwell, Sir Herbert	*The Life & Letters of the Fourth Earl of Clarendon.* 2 vols. 1913

Mitford, E. L. — *A Land March from England to Ceylon Forty Years Ago*. 2 vols. 1884

Moore, R. J. — *Sir Charles Wood's Indian Policy 1853-66*. 1966

Morison, J. L. — "From Alexander Burnes to Frederick Roberts," *Proc. of British Academy* XXII (1936) 177-206

Murray, Margaret — *My First Hundred Years*. 1963

Newby, Eric — *A Short Walk in the Hindu Kush*. 1958

Outram, Sir James — *Lieut.-General Sir James Outram's Persian campaign in 1857*. 1860. Privately printed

Pelly, Lewis — *Journal of a Journey from Persia to India through Herat and Candahar*. Bombay, 1866

Pollock, J. C. — *Way to Glory: the life of Havelock of Lucknow*. 1957

Pottinger, Henry — *Travels in Beloochistan and Sinde*. 1816

Purdon, H. G. — *Memoirs of the 64th Regiment*. 1882

Rawlinson, Sir Henry — *England and Russia in the East*. 1875

Sen, Surendra Nath — *Eighteen Fifty-Seven*. Calcutta 1958

Shakespear, Sir Richmond — "From Heraut to Ourenbourg," *Blackwood's Magazine*, June 1842

Sheil, Lady M. L. — *Glimpses of life and manners in Persia*. 1856

Shepherd, William A. — *From Bombay to Bushire and Bussora; including an account of the present state of Persia, and notes on the Persian War*. 1857

Sidebottom, John K. — *The Overland Mail. A Postal historical study of the mail route to India*. 1948

Smith, R. Bosworth — *Life of Lord Lawrence*. 2 vols. 1883

Smyth, Sir John — *The Story of the Victoria Cross*. 1963

Stewart, C. E. — *Through Persia in disguise, with reminiscences of the Indian Mutiny*. 1911

Sykes, Sir Percy M. — *A History of Afghanistan*. 2 vols. 1940

Thornton, A. P. — "British Foreign Policy in Persia, 1858-90," *English Historical Review*, LXIX (1954) 554-57

Trotter, Lionel J. — *History of India under Queen Victoria from 1836 to 1880*. 2 vols. 1886

Vambéry, Arminius — *Travels in Central Asia, Being an Account of a Journey from Teheran across the Turkoman Desert on the Eastern Shore of the Caspian to Khiva, Bokhara and Samarcand Performed in the Year 1863*. 1864

Vigne, Godfrey T. — *A Personal Narrative of a visit to Ghuzni, Kabul and Afghanistan, and of a Residence at the Court of Dost Mohammed with Notices of Runjit Sing, Khiva, and the Russian Expedition*. 1840

Wainwright, M. D. and Matthews, N. (eds). — *A Guide to Western Manuscripts and Documents in the British Isles relating to South and South East Asia*. 1965

Ward, Sir A. W. and Gooch, G. P. (eds.) — *The Cambridge History of British Foreign Policy, 1783-1919*. 3 vols. 1922-3

Ward, S. G. P. — *Faithful: The Story of the Durham Light Infantry*. 1963

Wilber, Donald N. — *Annotated Bibliography of Afghanistan*. 1956, New Haven, U.S.A.

Wilson, Sir Arnold T. — *A Bibliography of Persia*. 1930

Woodham-Smith, Cecil — *The Reason Why*. 1953

Woodruff, Philip — *The Men who ruled India*. 2 vols. 1953-4

Notes

CHAPTER I The fabled city of Herat

1 Fitzroy Maclean, *A Person from England,* 15-16

2 Rawlinson, *England and Russia in the East,* 63-4

3 Conolly, *Journey to the North of India,* I, 37, 285-6

4 Fitzroy Maclean, *A Person from England,* 17, 89

5 Ferrier, *Caravan Journeys,* Appendix F (525 n.)

6 Kaye, *War in Afghanistan,* I, 526 n.

7 Henry Pottinger, *Travels in Beloochistan and Sinde,* Appendix, 413-17. Christie was preceded by a Bengal Civil Servant in 1783-4: George Forster, *A Journey from Bengal to England,* 2 vols. 1798, 1808. For other travellers in Central Asia, see H. W. C. Davis, "The Great Game in Asia (1800-1844)," *Proceedings of the British Academy,* XII (1926), 229: Rawlinson, *England and Russia in the East,* 208-35: Grey & Garrett, *European Adventurers of Northern India 1785 to 1849*: Forrest, *Selections from the Travels and Journals Preserved in the Bombay Secretariat.*

8 Grey & Garrett, *op. cit.,* 265-91

9 Forrest, *op. cit.,* i, 8: Grey & Garrett, *op. cit.,* 148-60, xxvii-xlviii

10 Grey & Garrett, *op. cit.,* 123

11 Forrest, *op. cit.,* 131. Also Masson, *Narrative of Various Journeys in Balochistan,* etc., 309-10. Masson's MS. of some Afghan journeys is in the India Office Library, MSS.Eur.8.218 and some of his drawings of Afghanistan are there also (unfortunately not of Herat).

12 Forrest, *op. cit.*, 123
13 Kaye, *War in Afghanistan*, I, 168; Stirling's diary (part only) is in the Library of the Royal Geographical Society.
14 Malleson, *Herat*, 37; Conolly, *Journey to the North of India*, II, 3-4
15 Conolly, *Journey to the North of India*, II, 2-3: Kaye, *Lives of Indian Officers*, II, contains an account of Conolly: see also H. W. C. Davis, *art. cit.*, 243-4
16 Mohun Lal, *Journal of a Tour*, 276, 277
17 Ferrier, *Caravan Journeys*, 148
18 Kaye, *War in Afghanistan*, I, 213: Kaye, *Lives of Indian Officers*, II, contains an account of Pottinger. I am also indebted to Mr D. Gourlay for allowing me to see his unpublished B.Litt. thesis (Univ. of St Andrews) on Eldred Pottinger.
19 Kaye, *War in Afghanistan*, I, 215: see also for this campaign W. Habberton, *Anglo-Russian Relations concerning Afghanistan*, 10-19
20 Kaye, *op. cit.*, I, 216
21 Sir John McNeill (1795-1883) was a Scotsman, Edinburgh University M.D., who was originally appointed as surgeon to the legation at Teheran and rose to be envoy. He was later appointed Poor Law Commissioner for Scotland and took successful measures to prevent the potato famine in Scotland becoming the catastrophe it did in Ireland. He was subsequently appointed a commissioner to inquire into the supplies for the British Army in the Crimea.
22 Sykes, *History of Afghanistan*, II, 331
23 Canning Papers: Papers on Miscellaneous Subjects, 222 (3)
24 Forrest, *Selections from Travels*, 97
25 Ferrier, *Caravan Journeys*, 171-2, 525
26 Fitzroy Maclean, *A Person from England*, 17-110
27 Mitford, *A Land March*, II, 38-9, 72, 74
28 Ferrier, *Caravan Journeys*, 526

29 Kaye, *Lives of Indian Officers*, III, contains an account of D'Arcy Todd. The members of the Mission are named by Sir John Login in Ferrier, *op. cit.*, p. 526 n., as Capt. Edward Sanders, Bengal Engineers: Lieut. James Abbott, Bengal Artillery: Lieut. Richmond Shakespear, Bengal Artillery: Asst. Surgeon J. S. Login, Bengal Horse Artillery: Lieut. Charles Frederick North, Bombay Engineers: four European sergeants of whom only two (Cameron and O'Gorman) are named by Login.

30 Ferrier, *op. cit.*, 528 n.: Mitford, *A Land March*, II, 64-71: Login, *Sir John Login and Duleep Singh*, 28

31 *Blackwood's Magazine* June 1842, 692

32 Col. Abbott, in Canning Papers: Papers on Miscellaneous Subjects, 222

33 Kaye, *War in Afghanistan*, I, 585, quoting a letter from Major Todd.

34 Login, *Sir John Login and Duleep Singh*, 51

35 Ferrier, *op. cit.*, 526 n.

36 Palmerston to Shiel, 11th Oct. 1851, in *Correspondence relative to the engagement with Persia respecting Herat*, printed for the Foreign Office, 1857

37 J. P. Ferrier, a Frenchman who enlisted as a private soldier and after some distinguished service in Africa became attached to the Persian Army, rising to the honorary rank of Adjutant-General. At the time of his *Caravan Journeys* he was a private individual travelling to Lahore in search of a post with Ranjit Singh, Maharajah of the Punjab.

38 Ferrier, *op. cit.*, 170-5: MS. Report on the Fortifications of Herat, India Office, Secret Dept., Nos. 50 and 51 of 1840

39 Ferrier, *op. cit.*, 173

40 Kaye, *War in Afghanistan*, I, 209

41 Dalhousie Papers: 8/414

42 Canning Papers: Papers on Miscellaneous Subjects, 225 and 574: Dodd, *History of the Indian Revolt*, 578-9: *Frontier and*

Overseas Expeditions from India, VI, 224: text of agreement of 1853 in Rawlinson, *England and Russia in the East*, Appendix I, 366–7

43 Dalhousie Papers: 6/118

44 Canning Papers: Canning to President of Board of Control, 15a (17th May, 1856)

45 Canning Papers: Correspondence with Col. John Jacob (2 bound volumes).

CHAPTER 2 Murray in Teheran

1 Maxwell, *Murray*, 245

2 Maxwell, *Murray*, 56–7

3 Maxwell, *Murray*, 60

4 Maxwell, *Murray*, 63

5 Dalhousie Papers: 6/146/413½; Murray to Dalhousie, 3rd Dec., 1850

6 Dalhousie Papers: 4/164/2212; Murray to Dalhousie, 9th Sept., 1854

7 Maxwell, *Murray*, 262

8 Dalhousie Papers: 6/169/2734; Murray to Dalhousie, 25th July, 1855

9 Dalhousie Papers: 6/166/2461; Murray to Dalhousie, 5th Jan., 1854

10 Dalhousie Papers: 6/168/2664; Murray to Dalhousie, 5th May, 1855

11 Dalhousie Papers: 6/166/2461; Murray to Dalhousie, 5th Jan., 1854

12 Shepherd, *Bombay to Bushire*, 158–9

13 Dalhousie Papers: 6/168/2664; Murray to Dalhousie, 5th May, 1855

14 Gobineau, *Trois Ans en Asie*, I, 303–5

15 Dalhousie Papers: 6/168/2664; Murray to Dalhousie, 5th May, 1855

16 Dalhousie Papers: 6/169/2735; Murray to Dalhousie, 1st Sept., 1855
17 M. Gail, *Persia and the Victorians*, 56-7
18 This account of the case of Hashim Khan is mainly taken from Dalhousie Papers 8/170, "Papers relative to the withdrawal of H.M.'s Mission to Teheran," printed for the Foreign Office, 21st Feb., 1856. Supplemented by Murray's letters to Lord Elphinstone, India Office Library, MSS. Eur. F.87, Box 6
19 Dalhousie Papers: 6/179/3; Murray to Dalhousie, 1st Dec., 1855
20 Dalhousie Papers: 5/9; memorandum on the massacre of the Russian envoy, by Dr. John McNeill, 1829
21 Dalhousie Papers: 6/179/3; Murray to Dalhousie, 1st Dec., 1855
22 Dalhousie Papers: 6/179/3

CHAPTER 3 Dost Mohammed Khan at Kabul

1 Mohun Lal, *Life of Dost Mohammed Khan*, I, 21-4
2 Mohun Lal, *Life of Dost Mohammed Khan*, I, 28
3 Forrest, *Selections from Travels*, 115, from Masson.
4 Forrest, *op. cit.*, 115; also Masson, *Narrative of Various Journeys*, I, 252, etc.
5 Vigne, *A Personal Narrative*, 347 and frontispiece; see page 46
6 Vigne, *op. cit.*, 363
7 Kaye, *War in Afghanistan*, I, 165
8 Kaye, *War in Afghanistan*, I and II. Macrory, *Signal Catastrophe*.
9 Mohun Lal, *Life of Dost Mohammed Khan*, II, 494-5
10 Rawlinson, *England and Russia in the East*, 368
11 Canning Papers: Minute, 15th May, 1856
12 Canning Papers: Papers on Miscellaneous Subjects, 166
13 Fitzmaurice, *Granville*, I, 221

14 Canning Papers: Minute, 10th Sept., 1856

15 Canning Papers: Letters to the President of the Board of Control, 44; Papers on Miscellaneous Subjects, 95 and 574. Esan Khan was later murdered by two Persian soldiers.

16 Canning Papers: Papers on Miscellaneous Subjects, 226

17 R. Bosworth Smith, *Life of Lord Lawrence*, I, 518–19

18 Bosworth Smith, *op. cit.*, I, 512

19 Bosworth Smith, *op. cit.*, I, 523

20 Bosworth Smith, *op. cit.*, I, 525

21 Canning Papers: Letters to the Court of Directors, 31/23 (23rd Jan., 1857). Agreement in Rawlinson, *op. cit.*, 368–70

CHAPTER 4 India prepares for war

1 Letter from Viscountess Canning (the widow of George Canning) to her son. Lady Canning's Papers (the property of the Earl of Harewood) are deposited at Leeds, Sheepscar Library. This letter is undated and has no reference number.

2 Maclagan, *Clemency Canning*, 38

3 Dalhousie Papers: 6/118; Dalhousie to Harris, 8th Jan., 1856

4 Baird, *Letters of the Marquess of Dalhousie*, 369

5 Canning Papers: Papers on Miscellaneous Subjects, 145, 437

6 Fitzmaurice, *Granville*, I, 145

7 Canning Papers: Letters to the President of the Board of Control, 7: Canning to Vernon Smith, 22nd April, 1856

8 Canning Papers: Letters to the President of the Board of Control, 28: Canning to Vernon Smith, 8th August, 1856

9 Canning Papers: Letters to the President of the Board of Control, 71: Canning to Vernon Smith, 20th June, 1857

10 Fitzmaurice, *Granville*, I, 155

11 Fitzmaurice, *Granville*, I, 156

12 Canning Papers: Papers on Miscellaneous Subjects, 44

13 Canning Papers: Papers on Miscellaneous Subjects, 26a

14 Fitzmaurice, *Granville*, I, 145

15 Canning Papers: Letters to the President of the Board of Control, 15a: Canning to Vernon Smith, 17th May, 1856
16 Canning Papers: Letters from the Governor of Bombay, 15/31 (8th October, 1856) and 15/29 (1st October, 1856). For the Aga Khan, see also the memoirs of the late Aga Khan, *World Enough and Time* (1954)
17 Canning Papers: Papers on Miscellaneous Subjects, 52
18 Low, *History of the Indian Navy*, I, 504-20
19 Low, *op. cit.*, II, 97
20 Low, *op. cit.*, II, 110-11
21 Canning Papers: Letters from the Governor of Bombay, 15/42 (14th November, 1856)
22 Low, *History of the Indian Navy*, II, 340-1
23 Canning Papers: Letters to the President of the Board of Control, 28 (8th August, 1856). The exact number of troops engaged varies considerably in the different reports of the Government of India probably owing to the uncertainty about the combatant status of some of the personnel.
24 Fitzmaurice, *Granville*, I, 145
25 Canning Papers: Letters to the President of the Board of Control, 4 (8th April, 1856)
26 Canning Papers: Letter from Dunkellin to Lady Canning, 7th November, 1856
27 Lady Canning's Diary, April, 1857
28 Canning Papers: Letters from the Governor of Bombay, 15/26 (14th September, 1856)
29 Low, *History of the Indian Navy*, II, 350
30 Dalhousie Papers: 6/158/1625 and 6/167/2502
31 *The Times*, 2nd December, 1856 (from the *Bombay Times*)
32 Low, *History of the Indian Navy*, II, 232
33 Low, *op. cit.*, II, 382–3
34 Dalhousie Papers: 6/42/10 and Elphinstone Papers: Box 7A
35 Dalhousie Papers: 6/117
36 *Punch*, 15th November, 1856

37 Canning Papers: Lady Canning's Diary, 14th June, 1856

38 Canning Papers: Lord Dunkellin to Gregory, 20th September, 1856

39 An account of this is given by the late Dr Margaret Murray, in her autobiography *My First Hundred Years* (1963), 40-1: Dr Murray's father had been present at the sermon.

40 Francis William Brown of Elgin was the nephew of General Sir George Brown (1790-1865) one of the Crimean War generals.

41 Combe's Letters: 13th March, 1856

42 Combe's Letters: 25th September, 1856

43 Combe's Letters: 5th October, 1856

44 G. D. Barker, *Letters from Persia and India, 1857-1859*, xvii

45 Canning Papers: Letters from the Governor of Bombay, 15/25 (8th September, 1856)

46 Canning Papers: Letters from the Governor of Bombay, 15/37 (1st November, 1856), and Letters to the President of the Board of Control, 48 (8th January, 1857)

47 Canning Papers: Letters from the Governor of Bombay, 15/32 (9th September/October, 1856)

48 Canning Papers: Letters from the Governor of Bombay, 15/46 (19th December, 1856)

49 Canning Papers: Letters from the Governor of Bombay, 15/39 (8th November, 1856)

CHAPTER 5 The Persian War – Bushire

1 *Calcutta Gazette Extraordinary:* a copy in Canning Papers: Papers on Miscellaneous Subjects, 225

2 Canning Papers: Letters from the Governor of Bombay, 15/45 (9th December, 1856)

3 Gobineau, *Trois Ans en Asie*, II, 15

4 Lady Sheil, *Glimpses of life and manners in Persia*, 94

5 Lady Sheil, *op. cit.*, 165

6 Lady Sheil, *op. cit.*, 141-2

7 Quoted by R. L. Greaves, *Persia and the Defence of India*, 9

8 Canning Papers: Papers on Miscellaneous Subjects, 437 – "Position and Policy of England as an Asiatic Power, 1855, printed only for the use of the Cabinet."

9 Lady Sheil, *op. cit.*, 88

10 Canning Papers: Letter of Dunkellin to Gregory, 4th March, 1857

11 Elphinstone Papers: Leeke to Elphinstone, 23rd November, 1856

12 Hunt, *Outram & Havelock's Persian Campaign*, 195

13 *Illustrated London News*, 4th April, 1857

14 Shepherd, *From Bombay to Bushire*, 220

15 The description of the landing at Halilah Bay and the battles of Reshire and Bushire is based on the despatches of General Stalker, Admiral Leeke and Commander Jones, all printed in *Outram's Persian Campaign in 1857*, 11-20: Ballard, *Blackwood's*, 1861: Purdon, *Memoirs of the 64th Regiment: Illustrated London News*, 7th February, 1857 and 4th April, 1857: Bell, *Account of the Wars with Persia:* MS. letters and diaries, especially that of Lt. F. W. Brown.

16 Probably built during the Dutch occupation of Karrack, *c.* 1760

17 Lt. Brown's letter of 12th December, 1856

18 *Illustrated London News*, 7th February, 1857

19 Combe's letter of 15th December, 1856

20 Ballard, *Blackwood's*, 1861, 349

21 Despatch of Commander Jones to the Bombay Government, printed in *Outram's Persian Campaign in 1857*, 18

22 *Frontier and Overseas Expeditions from India*, VI, 227-8

23 Canning Papers: Letter of Dunkellin to Lady Canning, 16th December, 1856

24 Shepherd, *From Bombay to Bushire*, 138-9

25 Gobineau, *Trois Ans en Asie*, I, 134-5

26 Canning Papers: Lady Canning's Diary, 25th Dec., 1857 [*sic*]
27 Canning Papers: Letters to the Court of Directors, 31/19 (8 Jan. 1857)
28 Elphinstone Papers: Murray to Elphinstone, 11th January, 1857
29 Canning Papers: Lord Dunkellin to Lady Canning, 16th December, 1856
30 Shepherd, *From Bombay to Bushire*, 231
31 Canning Papers: Lord Dunkellin to Lady Canning, 16th December, 1856
32 Combe's Letters: 21st July, 1857
33 Combe's Letters: 5th January, 1857. Ballard, *Blackwood's*, 1861, 352-3. Ballard dates this incident Christmas Eve-Christmas Day, but Combe, writing four days later, and not four years later, is almost certain to be right about the date.
34 Dalhousie Papers: 6/519
35 Canning Papers: Governor-General's Register of Letters Received, 456

CHAPTER 6 The Persian War – Khoosh-ab

1 Canning Papers: Letters from the Governor of Bombay, 15/39 (8th November, 1856)
2 Canning Papers: Lady Canning's Diary, 2nd May, 1856
3 Goldsmid, *Outram*, II, 130
4 Canning Papers: Letters to the President of the Board of Control, 45 (7th December, 1856)
5 Goldsmid, *Outram*, II, 130 n.
6 See page 78
7 Maclagan, *Clemency Canning*, 122
8 Maclagan, *loc. cit.*, and Hare, *Two Noble Lives*, II, 252-3
9 Pollock, *Way to Glory*, 22-32, etc.
10 Maclagan, *Clemency Canning*, 295 & n.

11 Dalhousie Papers: 8/332, Ellenborough to Panmure, 11th July, 1857

12 Canning Papers: Letters to the President of the Board of Control, 9 (23rd April, 1856)

13 Pollock, *Way to Glory*, 7

14 For the evils of the purchase system, see Woodham Smith, *The Reason Why*.

15 Marshman, *Havelock*, 209

16 Hare, *Two Noble Lives*, II, 363, quoting Lady Canning's Diary, 27th November, 1857

17 Marshman, *Havelock*, 237

18 Havelock-Allan Papers: Letters to his wife, various dates.

19 Lambrick, *John Jacob of Jacobabad*, 316–17: Jacob's Diary, 19th January, 1857

20 Later General Sir George Digby Barker, G.C.B., Governor of the Bermudas, etc. His letters were published in 1915, edited by Lady Barker.

21 Barker, *op. cit.*, frontispiece.

22 Barker, *op. cit.*, xiv-xvi

23 Barker, *op. cit.*, 3–4

24 Hunt, *Outram & Havelock's Persian Campaign*. Barker, *op. cit.*, 9

25 Borthwick, letter of 19th January, 1857

26 Hunt, *op. cit.*, 198

27 Dalhousie Papers: 6/519, copy of Outram's despatch: also *Outram's Persian Campaign*, 30

28 Dalhousie Papers: 6/519

29 Barker, *Letters from Persia and India*, 14

30 Barker, *loc. cit.*

31 Combe's Letters: 12th February, 1857

32 Hunt, *Outram & Havelock's Persian Campaign*, 211

33 Combe's Letters: 12th February, 1857

34 Hunt, *op. cit.*, 214–15

35 Canning Papers: Papers on Miscellaneous Subjects, 419

36 *Illustrated London News*, 18th April, 1857; Combe's Letters: 12th February, 1857

37 Although this was said at the time of the Persian campaign, in fact the Lancers broke a square in the Punjab War at Aliwal in 1846: and the Light Dragoons did so at Salamanca in 1812 (Marquess of Anglesey, ed., *Sergeant Pearman's Memoirs*, 22–3, 45)

38 Smyth, *The Story of the Victoria Cross*, 100. Gazetted, 3rd August, 1860

39 Hunt,. *op. cit.*, 218

40 Hunt, *op. cit.*, 220–1; Combe's Letters: 12th February, 1857; Dalhousie Papers: 6/519

41 Dalhousie Papers: 6/519 (letters from Outram)

42 Borthwick's Letters: 15th Feb. and 4th March, 1857

43 Stewart, *Through Persia in disguise*, 88

44 Canning Papers: Papers on Miscellaneous Subjects, 124, 124A; Dalhousie Papers: 6/519

45 Borthwick's Letters: 4th March, 1857

CHAPTER 7 The Persian War – Mohammerah

1 Hunt, *Outram & Havelock's Persian Campaign*, 235

2 Havelock's Letters: to his wife, 1st March, 1857

3 Borthwick's Letters: 4th March, 1857

4 Dalhousie Papers: 6/519

5 Hunt, *op. cit.*, 230

6 Jacob's Diary: 16th March, 1857; Lambrick, *John Jacob of Jacobabad*, 321

7 Jacob's Diary: 15th March, 1857; Lambrick, *op. cit.*, 320–1

8 Dalhousie Papers: 6/519; Elphinstone Papers: Letters from General Stalker to Elphinstone.

9 Dalhousie Papers: 6/519

10 India Office Records, Enclosures to Military Letters from Bombay, Vol. 29: Inquest on Major-General Stalker. Also

Canning Papers: Lady Canning's Diary, April, 1857. Surgeon Mills was one of three appointed to investigate Stalker's death.

11 Jacob's Diary: 15th March, 1857; Lambrick, *op. cit.*, 320

12 Jacob's Diary: 17th March, 1857

13 Jacob's Diary: 17th March, 1857; Lambrick, *op. cit.*, 321

14 *Saturday Review*, 23rd May, 1857

15 Ballard, *Blackwood's*, 1861, 351

16 In the eighteenth century, the river Karun (a Persian river) had entered the Persian Gulf by several outlets, the main one being the Bahmishir. But in 1765 a canal had been cut from the Karun to the Shatt-al-Arab (a Turkish river which was the combined Tigris and Euphrates rivers) and eventually the main body of water of the Karun came through this canal, which was called the Hafar. Mohammerah was built on the Hafar and thus commanded the entrances of three very important rivers, the Tigris, the Euphrates and the Karun.

17 Hunt, *op. cit.*, 263 and *Illustrated London News*, 23rd May, 1857

18 Dalhousie Papers: 6/519; Low, *History of the Indian Navy*, II, 359

19 Low, *op. cit.*, II, 403-6

20 Low, *op. cit.*, II, 351

21 Lambrick, *John Jacob of Jacobabad*, 321-2, and Low, *op. cit.*, II, 351 n.

22 *Outram's Persian Campaign*, 204-5. Mohammerah had been occupied in 1841 by the Persians and by agreement between the Russians and the British Persia had been allowed to keep it. N. Kubie, *Road to Nineveh* (*The Adventures and Excavations of Sir Austen Henry Layard*), 137-9

23 *Outram's Persian Campaign*, 163

24 Havelock Papers: Memorandum on the operations at Mohammerah, 13th March, 1857. Marshman, *Havelock*, 240-1

25 Barker, *Letters from Persia and India*, 26. (He did survive and became a general.)

26 Hunt, *Outram & Havelock's Persian Campaign*, 248
27 Low, *History of the Indian Navy*, II, 360. From the account of the battle by Lt. A. Stiffe, I.N., in the *Bombay Gazette*, 2nd June, 1857
28 Low, *op. cit.*, II, 355
29 Hunt, *op. cit.*, 249-50
30 *Illustrated London News*, 23rd May, 1857
31 Hunt, *op. cit.*, 251-2
32 Lambrick, *John Jacob of Jacobabad*, 323
33 Combe's Letters: 31st May, 1857
34 Borthwick's Letters: 12th April, 1857
35 Hunt, *op. cit.*, 259
36 Hunt, *op. cit.*, chapter VII. Barker, *op. cit.*, 27-30
37 Borthwick's Letters: 12th April, 1857
38 Hunt, *op. cit.*, 300
39 Havelock Papers: Letter to his wife dated 5th April, 1857. Marshman, *Havelock*, 246
40 Curzon, *Persia*, II, 339-40 n.

CHAPTER 8 Peace

1 Maxwell, *Clarendon*, II, 107
2 Fitzmaurice, *Granville*, I, 145
3 *Quarterly Review*, April, 1857, 534. It seems probable that this information came from Mr. Layard.
4 *Quarterly Review*, April, 1857, 535
5 *Quarterly Review*, April, 1857, 536
6 *Quarterly Review*, January, 1857, 250
7 Maxwell, *Clarendon*, II, 138
8 *Hansard*, 3rd February, 1857, col. 125
9 *Hansard*, 13th February, 1857, col. 625
10 *Saturday Review*, May, 1857
11 *Illustrated London News*, 14th February, 1857
12 *Saturday Review*, March, 1857

13 The full text of the treaty can be found in Rawlinson, *England and Russia in the East*, Appendix 4, 370–3
14 Borthwick's Letters: 12th April, 1857
15 *Outram's Campaign*, 265
16 Barker, *Letters from Persia and India*, 36
17 *Outram's Campaign*, 280
18 This frank is on a letter from Pelly at Mohammerah to Jacob at Bushire, India Office Home Miscellaneous, vol. 550, 1169
19 Bell, *Account of British Wars with Persia*, 55
20 Barker, *Letters from Persia and India*, 36, 40
21 *Outram's Campaign*, 291
22 Hunt, *Outram & Havelock's Persian Campaign*, 329: Barker, *op. cit.*, 35. Hunt returned to India and died of cholera in 1858.
23 *Outram's Campaign*, 270
24 *Outram's Campaign*, 299. Lord Dunkellin returned to India to find himself elected as Member of Parliament for the town of Galway by his father's respectful tenants. He later became Member for Galway County, and died aged 40, in 1867, of a kidney disease contracted during the Persian war.
25 Lambrick, *John Jacob of Jacobabad*, 326–7
26 *Outram's Campaign*, 299
27 India Office Records, Home Miscellaneous, 550, 9th May, 1857
28 *Outram's Campaign*, 322
29 Canning Papers: Papers on Miscellaneous Subjects, 419; *Outram's Campaign*, 368–9, 375
30 All gazetted 3.8.1860
31 L. L. Gordon, *British Battles and Medals*, 232–3; also S. G. P. Ward, *Faithful*, 231
32 *Outram's Campaign*.
33 Havelock Papers: Letter to his wife, 31st May, 1857
34 *Outram's Campaign*, 354–5
35 Maclagan, *Clemency Canning*, 79 n.
36 *Outram's Campaign*, 378

37 India Office Records, Home Miscellaneous, 550, 1455, letter from Jones to Jacob; also Canning Papers: Papers on Miscellaneous Subjects, 296

38 Dr S. N. Sen (*Eighteen Fifty-Seven*) in the best modern account of the Mutiny deals with the alleged Persian plot, 403-5

39 India Office Records, Home Miscellaneous, 550, letter, 10th May, 1857

40 Canning Papers: Murray to Canning, 17th October, 1857

41 Canning Papers: Papers on Miscellaneous Subjects, 574; also Eastwick, *Journal of a Diplomate's three years' residence in Persia*, I, 239

42 C. E. Stewart, *Through Persia in disguise*, 221

43 Canning Papers: Report from Taylor to the Government of India Foreign Office, 12th November, 1857

44 Canning Papers: Report from Rawlinson to the Foreign Office, No. 7, 26th February, 1860

45 Canning Papers: *loc. cit.* Taylor became Political Agent at Jeypore, 1858-9, and Meywar, 1859-62, and retired a colonel in 1865, dying in 1906, aged 84. For the plot to overthrow Ahmed Khan see also Pelly's papers, F.O. 800/233, No. 1912, and Pelly's *Journal of a Journey from Persia to India*. The pretender was a brother of Ahmed Khan.

46 Vambéry, *Travels in Central Asia*, 7, 269-85. Vambery arrived in Herat two months after the city was taken, and the city and the country for miles around had been devastated.

47 Jacob's Diary: 29th September, 1857

48 Jacob's Diary: 1st-2nd October, 1857. Jacob was to be offered the command of the Central India Force, but as he did not reach India in time it was given to Rose. Jacob died in 1858, of sunstroke brought on by excessive heat and overwork.

49 India Office: Home Miscellaneous, 550, Letter from Jones to Jacob, 13th October, 1857

Index

INDEX

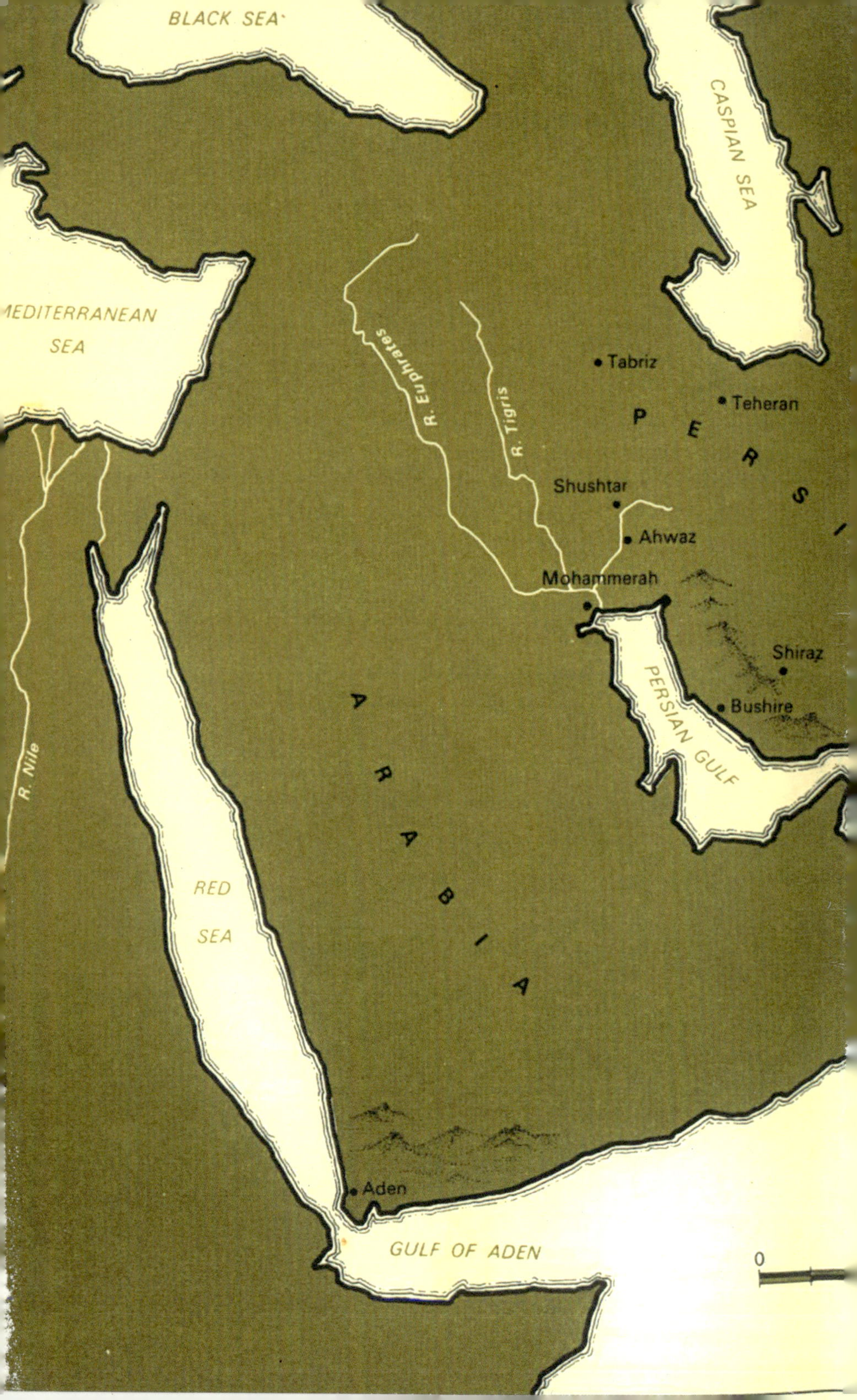
BLACK SEA
CASPIAN SEA
MEDITERRANEAN SEA
R. Euphrates
R. Tigris
Tabriz
Teheran
PERSI
Shushtar
Ahwaz
Mohammerah
Shiraz
Bushire
PERSIAN GULF
ARABIA
R. Nile
RED SEA
Aden
GULF OF ADEN
0